Survival

Of

A

Spirit

7-30-95

to Pat and Frank

Eva Salin

Survival

Of

A

Spirit

written and illustrated
by

EVA SALIER

SHENGOLD PUBLISHERS, INC.
New York

Dedicated to my late husband, Max, and
to our children and their children

ISBN 0-88400-180-6
Library of Congress Catalog Card Number: 95-067140
Copyright © 1995 by Eva Salier

Published by Shengold Publishers, Inc.
18 West 45th Street
New York, NY 10036
Printed in the United States of America

Contents

Foreword vi

Chapter 1. Happy Childhood 1

Chapter 2. Hell-bound 7

Chapter 3. Vught 15

Chapter 4. Many Deaths and a Tiny Satisfaction 23

Chapter 5. End of Children; Philips 28

Chapter 6. Auschwitz-Birkenau 39

Chapter 7. 1940 52

Chapter 8. Reichenbach 59

Chapter 9. Bombs and Beets 66

Chapter 10. Christmas 1944 78

Chapter 11. Across and Inside Mountains 89

Chapter 12. Beendorf and Gypsies 101

Chapter 13. May 1, 1945 111

Epilogue 121

Glossary:

Obersturmbannführer = lieutenant colonel

Scharführer = noncommissioned rank

Untersturmführer = second lieutenant

SS (Schutzstaffel) = Defense Echelon

Foreword

What is both remarkable and delightful about Eva Salier, who wrote and illustrated *Survival of a Spirit*, is her ability to rejoice in every manifestation of the better side of human nature, however brief and limited it may be, and to explain human frailties and failings without bitterness or anger. It is that unique characteristic that underscores her autobiographical work and embodies its title.

She was probably born an artist and has been an accomplished painter, mostly in water colors, since her arrival in southern New Jersey. All her life she has honed her skills and power of observation while reading voraciously on a wide range of subjects to satisfy her hunger for knowledge.

A widowed mother of two sons, one a film editor in Hollywood, the other an archaeologist, she is kept busy advising a local theater company, serving as the chief graphic artist and designer for a weekly newspaper and as a writer. She wishes she had more time for two of her many hobbies: Classical music and gardening.

Eva Salier's experience and endurance during the Holocaust have tempered and purified her character and emotional stability the way a furnace tempers steel and renders it strong and resilient. Endowed with a sense of humor, she shuns publicity and downplays her courage in the face of the Nazi barbarisms of the Final Solution. She eschews generalities, has little patience with mediocrity, and tends to speak her mind bluntly. She has an enormous circle of friends.

Survival of a Spirit began as a personal memoir intended only for her children and grandchildren. Several readings by literary editors and critics, all of whom praised it, led her to embark on rewriting and enlarging it. The book is an authentic and true chronicle of Eva Salier's escapes from being murdered in the Holocaust.

—*Alex Urban*

Chapter 1

Happy Childhood

I was a happy child, and I had every reason to be one.

I was born in Germany in 1923, five years after the end of World War 1, when the world seemed to be coming out of its postwar depression even while—although people were unaware of it then—the foundation for the next world war was being laid.

I was the only child of loving, intelligent, and fairly well-to-do parents. My father was Dutch and Mother was German. Father had an import-and-export business and had bought a house in Horchheim, a suburb of Koblenz on the Rhine, so that he could supervise the unpacking and repacking of the cheese, butter, and sugar he imported while they were checked at the customs authority in Koblenz.

Being a bachelor, he had a housekeeper, Frau Knopp, who looked after the house when he was "not in residence" as well as after him when he was.

He was a smallish man and very vivacious. He had a full, reddish mustache, which compensated for his almost complete baldness. He was in his late forties when he married Mother.

Daddy had a definite sense of humor, and there always seemed to be a twinkle in his blue eyes. He could and often did keep sizable audiences in stitches. He composed outrageous songs for all occasions and wrote them on whatever happened to be handy: tablecloths, napkins, and even curtains. He loved to poke fun at the ponderous, titled Germans and did so to their faces. His charm protected him from reprisals.

He loved to play with me and all my friends, and to them he was Uncle Hellendag. He showed us how to climb trees, skip rope, and play a mean game of marbles.

He had his clothes tailor-made in England, mostly gray or dark blue pin-striped vested suits that he wore with high, stiff collars and soft, rather flamboyant ties with a large tiepin. And though I loved him dearly, I was a bit embarrassed by his appearance, because it differed so radically from that of other fathers. I always hoped that he wouldn't be noticed by my classmates when he came to my school to play chess with our principal, which happened often.

He also played the piano, and if he heard a melody once, he could play it. When my parents returned home from an opera or operetta, I would be treated to the wonderful music even when I was supposed to be sleeping. He had a talent that I am sorry to say I did not inherit.

My mother was a beautiful woman, slightly taller than father and twenty years his junior. Her jet-black hair, short and combed simply back from her high forehead, and almost violet blue eyes were startling. She had a statuesque figure and knew how to dress. She was an elegant woman who carried herself with a natural grace.

Mother was one of the most intelligent women I have ever known, and her interests were so varied that one would have been hard pressed to find a subject that she did not know something about or did not arouse a curiosity in her. She was a voracious reader and blessed with a prodigious memory; she could recall almost verbatim whatever she had just read. I am still in awe that she knew by heart much of Goethe, Schiller, and Shakespeare. At a time when it was less common than it is today for a woman to study, she did. She could also do the most intricate handcrafts, loved to knit and embroider, and she played the violin.

Our house was on the Chaussee (Embankment), a street that ran parallel to the Rhine and was so named since the French occupation of the Rhineland after World War 1. Its original name was Koblenzer Strasse (Koblenz Street) and it was considered the most elegant avenue of this suburb of Koblenz.

The houses stood far apart from each other in well-tended gardens, overflowing with flowers, fruit trees, and vegetables. Ours was a three-story house of yellowish brick, a slate roof, and many high windows with dark green working shutters. The entrance was formal but not forbidding. The walls were so thick that when my parents wanted to install central-heating ducts throughout the house, it could not be done. The deep—and for me, when I was small, spooky—vaulted cellar was truly a wine cellar, always well stocked.

The rooms with their parquet floors and oriental carpets were comfortably furnished. My bedroom was on the third floor and looked out onto the back garden. The most vivid memory I have of this room is the view from my bed of the uppermost branches of a large cherry tree.

I loved that tree. In the spring it looked like a bride in its white blossom gown. Then, in the summer, when the heavy foliage stepped on the white blossoms, it would hide me while I sat crouched on a branch with my back leaning against the comforting trunk reading and, when ripe, enjoying handfuls of cherries. I was always sad when fall stripped the branches of their leaves. But then came winter with a white snow blanket and the promise of another spring.

Outside the entrance to my room was a sort of a balcony overlooking the second floor. When my parents had one of their musical evenings, mother playing the violin, father at the piano, and two or three friends making up a quartet or quintet performing Schubert, Mozart, or Haydn, I would sit on the floor of that balcony with my legs dangling between the bars of the handrail and listen. My legs, of course, gave me away.

The front yard was a sea of flowers while in the rear, behind the house, was an enormous fruit and vegetable garden, and all of it was my mother's joy and pride, which she kept blooming and bountiful with the help of Zeppl. Zeppl was a Tyrolean gardener who walked in one day looking for a meal while on his way to Hamburg and from there to America. He stayed on for the rest of his life.

Behind the house in the courtyard stood my little playhouse. Father, with the help of Zeppl, had built it out of a large crate in which a tractor from America had been shipped. It was a masterpiece with two windows and a door and was painted in bright colors. It was also furnished and was the attraction of all the neighborhood kids. We often had impromptu picnics in there and played in it when the weather was bad.

Naturally, there was every chance that as an only child I would be a spoiled one. But Käthe, our housekeeper and general factotum, saw to it that this would not happen.

She was the daughter of my father's housekeeper, Mrs. Knopp, while he was still a bachelor, as I mentioned before, and stayed on when he and Mother got married. When I was on the way, my parents looked for a nurse-maid, and Mrs. Knopp's daughter—Kätta as her mother called her—was the natural choice. She was sixteen at the time, and we grew up together.

My father not only was no disciplinarian but, on the contrary, he liked all my tomboy activities and even egged me on. Mother was a bit stricter in that respect but it was Käthe who made sure that my misdeeds didn't go unpunished. She was the one who gave me a good spanking when I deserved it or let me stand in a corner to contemplate my "crimes." She made sure that I never had those privileges that most "only" children had. I loved her deeply.

Our home was a religious one. My grandfather on father's side had been a Torah soifer (a scribe of the scrolls of the Torah), who did it not as a profession but rather as a mitzvah, a good deed. Grandmother was the business woman. Father, naturally, spoke not only fluent German, English, and Dutch, but also French and Hebrew.

Sabbath was strictly observed, and although it was more than an hour's walk to the synagogue in Koblenz, we rarely missed a service. I would never dream of doing any manual work on the Sabbath like drawing or sewing. Instead my parents and I took long walks, sometimes with friends, or we visited them in Koblenz. And we read. And we ate strictly kosher, and Käthe, who was Catholic, was the most fanatic observer of kashruth. I was allowed to invite as many of my non-Jewish friends as I wished to share the Jewish holidays with us and I was always welcomed to spend Christmas and Easter at their homes. Those were the days.

My parents were well respected both in Koblenz and in Horchheim. They were very hospitable, and our house was always filled with company, Jews and Christians from all walks of life. Like my parents, I also had many friends, and either they were in our house or I was in theirs. Everybody watched each others' children, and it was a sunny and carefree existence.

I went to the small village school of Horchheim where the classes were large—sixty kids in first grade. But we all respected the teachers, and our parents were solidly behind them. We knew we had better pay attention, behave ourselves, and learn. I was the only Jewish child in my class, but the only time it made any difference was during the Jewish High Holidays when I went to the synagogue instead of the school.

After four years in the village school, at the age of ten, I was sent in 1933 to the *Gymnasium* (high school) in Koblenz. It was a very demanding and highly desirable school with a tough entrance exam. I was accepted, and quite proud of it. Classes were small, with about twenty-four students, the curriculum was intense—we studied French, biology, physics, chemistry, geometry, history, etc.—and there was never a question of what you wanted to study. Regardless of what your favorite subjects were, you had to participate in all. All the teachers had Ph.D.'s and were highly professional.

In the spring, and as long as the weather was warm, I bicycled there. Sometimes I crossed the river on a boat and walked the rest of the way. In the winter, or in bad weather, I took a commuter train into Koblenz.

Slowly but surely, dark clouds began to gather on my sunny life, and the ominous shadow of Nazism and Hitler started to stretch across the landscape. It took some time for the shadow to reach me in the *Gymnasium*, and the first two years in that school in Koblenz were great. I had made many new friends, I liked the school and my teachers, and, above all, enjoyed the challenge of the broad curriculum.

By the time I was twelve and in the third year of the *Gymnasium*, the long dark shadow finally reached the school. Our biology classes were discontinued and replaced by *Rassenkunde* (race science), the study of racial differences.

My parents, seeing the handwriting on the wall with its ever darker menace and my growing unhappiness in school, decided to leave Germany. Father had many business associates in England and was negotiating with an Englishman to buy into a factory in Richmond near London. But in the summer of 1935, before the deal went through, my father died. He left my mother, who was devastated, and me, who had idolized him, and both of us had a terrible time trying to adjust to the fact of his death while shivering in Hitler's cold and all-pervasive presence.

Käthe, who had left us to get married and by now had a small daughter, moved back into our house with her husband and child to be of help to us. It was more than mere help; it gave both my mother and me enormous support, because we not only had to wrestle with the tragic loss of my father, but we also began to experience great disappointments all around us.

It didn't take long for our friends and neighbors to shun us. I realize now that it was out of fear, but at the time it was unbelievably hurtful. The homes that had always been open and welcoming to us were suddenly hermetically sealed. Here and there a brave soul made an attempt to maintain the friendship, but only when nobody else was looking, or the darkness of the night made detection difficult. Some remained good friends and didn't worry about the consequences, and Käthe was one of them, and I have never forgotten it.

My school, the *Gymnasium*, which I had loved so much, became a place to be dreaded. It took all my courage even to enter the building. One other youngster and I were the only two Jewish kids in my class, and we were ordered to sit in the back row, by ourselves, never to raise our hands, to talk only when we were asked to do so, and we were called *die Unkräuter* (the weeds). It was a terrible year and a half that I spent in this once beloved school with girls around me who at one time, not so long ago, had been my friends and now had turned into my enemies.

Finally, in my fourth year of the *Gymnasium*, all the Jewish students were expelled and that school was declared *judenrein* (free of Jews).

Late in the summer of 1936, Mother sent me to live with our family in Amsterdam. I was thirteen years old and at a stage of adolescent life which, in the best of circumstances, is difficult.

I came to live with an aunt and uncle and two cousins, both boys, one six months older than I and the other a year younger. Their apartment in a lovely section of Amsterdam was spacious. I was enrolled in an industrial high school, and Mother stayed behind in Germany to go back to a university to get her degree in podiatry and to sell the house and father's warehouse.

The change from my life in Horchheim with its horrors and fear of Hitler to this seemingly untouched life in Amsterdam was bewildering. I could not understand how my family here could be so completely ignorant of what was happening so close by them. They had no understanding of the trauma I had experienced and was still going through.

Aunt and uncle were a unit by themselves. Their life was busy with travel, theater, opera, and all the activities that had for some time been forbidden to the Jews in Germany. We, the three youngsters, were more or less left to our own devices. I grew very close to my younger cousin, who seemed a bit more sensitive about my feelings than the rest of the family. Also, the cook, Hedwig, felt somewhat sorry for me, and she talked and, more importantly, listened to me.

The industrial school was very different from the *Gymnasium*, and at first I really felt like a fish out of water. It did not take me too long, however, to make new friends, and here I must say that I made good and lifelong friends. But I missed my mother, Käthe and her family as well as the few friends that had the courage to remain friends. I also missed the more challenging *Gymnasium* but only until the moment I got into the industrial school's art department. From then on I was perfectly happy with the school. We had good, even famous teachers, and I made great strides.

About a year and a half later, in 1938, my mother emigrated to the Netherlands. She really wanted to get out of Europe but our Dutch family persuaded her to settle there. Why not? they asked. Nothing was going to happen there. Were they ever wrong!

Mother had to take her exams in Dutch, and during that time she lived in Den Haag, the Hague. When she moved finally to Amsterdam and opened an office there, I moved in with her, of course. My aunt and uncle with their two sons, all still oblivious to the dangers lurking across the border, moved to France where uncle started the Oranje ("orange" in Dutch) Film Company.

Mother's great worries were to get her sisters, brothers, and her mother out of Hitler's Third Reich while at the same time starting her practice. It was a tough time, and it took a heavy toll on her.

Finally Grandmother joined us. Sadly, she was a very negative woman and even as a little girl I had promised myself never to be like her. Our life became unpleasant, and in Germany the Führer was expanding his Reich, and on May 10, 1940, the Netherlands was invaded by the Nazi hordes, and after five days the blitzkrieg had successfully gobbled up that little nation. From then on, my trip to that particular hell now called the Holocaust began.

Chapter 2

Hell-bound

It was spring again, 1943, but now I was standing with a group of women and other teenaged girls in front of a wooden barrier. We were carrying knapsacks, backpacks, pillowcases and even suitcases that contained all our earthly possessions. We were all workers from Hirsch's, originally a famous department store in Amsterdam which the Nazis had confiscated from its Jewish owners and converted into a slave-labor factory. But at this moment we were a raggedy and forlorn group that had just spent four days and nights in the Schouwburg, a famous theater in Amsterdam which had been converted by the Nazis into a temporary holding pen for the Jews who were to be transported either to Westerborg or to Vught. Westerborg was the *Durchgangslager,* a transient camp, Vught was the concentration camp in the Netherlands. The Schouwburg is now, so many years later, a monument, its outer walls still standing and inside a beautiful sculpture memorializing the Holocaust. But then it was the beginning of our trip through hell. From there we were transported by train to Vught, 55 kilometers (33 miles) from the German border. The train ride took about two hours and now we were here—at the barrier, the entrance to the camp.

We were dead tired. I was so tired that I don't even remember whether I was also hungry. The previous four days, spent at the once beautiful Schouwburg theater, were exhausting. The Shouwburg was so jam packed—even by Nazi standards—that we spent the first night across the street in some private homes requisitioned by the Nazis, and even there the sheer number of us, an overflow of humanity, filled every available space on beds, chairs, and floors. And the threat of air raids meant we could not use lights after dark. Thus we were crammed together in total darkness and spent the night sitting on any available piece of furniture or floor.

Next morning we were taken across the street back to the Schouwburg where the overcrowding had temporarily eased as a result of the transfer of most of the previous arrivals to their final destination. We, however, remained in the dark about our fate. My most vivid memory of that place was the painful inadequacy of toilet facilities, which the architect of this palace of entertainment could never have anticipated. Waiting in line for the men's and ladies' bathrooms was now a full-time occupation. As soon as one had finally been successful and had also avoided being pushed or pulled from one's place in the line, it was right back to the end of the line to start all over.

While waiting, we killed time by sitting and even stretching out on the floor, chatting, visiting each other and trying to keep up each other's spirits. We were, after all, a small group of young girls and women who had become friends while serving as slave laborers to the Nazis, sewing and making fur coats and hats for the German troops on the Russian front. Since our deportation, we had stayed together. Now, waiting in that never-ending line to the bathrooms, huddled somewhere under a balcony of the Schouwburg, a theater emptied of all the seats to make more room in what had become an enormous cavern, we observed an elderly man, very upset, approach us with tears streaming down his face. He carried a prayerbook. In a shaking and barely audible voice, he said in Yiddish, *"Denk nur hat sich gekummen die Fanya, hat sich gemolden freiwillig.* [Can you imagine that Fanya came and gave herself up]."

He did not know us, and we didn't know him but later on we met Fanya. She was his daughter and had been in hiding. Word had reached her hiding place that her parents and older sister had been picked up by the Nazis, whereupon she decided to come out of hiding to be with them. Only Fanya and her sister made it with us to the Vught camp.

Also with us was a young couple with three small children, two girls with long hair and a boy, well-behaved and beautiful kids with large dark eyes. Their mother, whose first name was Wiesje, had worked with us at Hirsch. I can still see her sitting on an old suitcase, cradling her son, embracing the girls, reassuring them with fairy tales and lulling them to sleep with soft songs. But the ominous setting for this scene in the converted playhouse was frightening and heartbreaking. Tragedy was wherever one looked, so numbing, incomprehensible and hopeless that all one could do—instinctively and in self-preservation—was to shut one's mind to it. One could not bear thinking or feeling.

After four nights it was finally our turn to leave the Schouwburg. Our herd of some 200 was taken at night by streetcar to the train station. It was at night that the Gestapo took over the streets and public transportation in that part of Amsterdam, where the general population of the city was always barred, specifically for the purpose of getting rid of the Jewish inhabitants with a minimum of fuss and attention. It was late at night when we entered the railroad station. A passenger train was waiting for us and the moment the last of us had been shouted at and shoved in, it departed.

Up to that moment we had no idea where we were being taken. A Dutch railroad employee, walking through the train, told us we were on our way to Vught, some two hours away. It was still dark outside when the train pulled into the tiny terminal there. We piled out and schlepped our pitiful belongings, prodded along by uniformed guards toward the camp.

And so, at last, we found ourselves standing in front of the wooden barrier that early spring dawn. And we remained standing. And we stood. And stood. And stood some more. After a long wait—there were always long waits; maybe that's why, even today, I still hate to wait—the gate opened, and we shuffled inside. We were now in the Vught concentration camp, and the gate closed behind us. As time passed, the names and locations of concentration camps kept changing but the barriers and the gates were always there, and they always closed behind those of us who had managed to survive yet one more camp.

We didn't even realize at this moment how lucky we were, the ones entering Vught. It turned out to be one of the "better" concentration camps, one that gave us a foretaste of what was to come. Meanwhile,

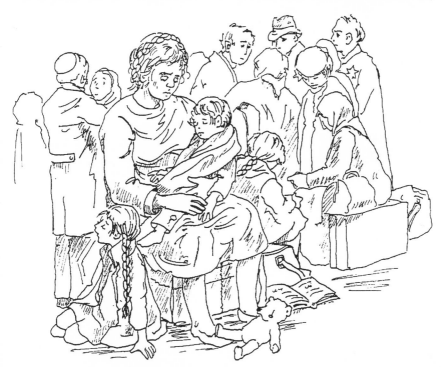

The young mother, Wiesje, with her three small children.

though, Vught consisted of rows and rows of barracks, red brick, straight neat roads leading to them, a big building (the kitchen), in the background the gray buildings of the *Industriehof* (industrial complex), and barbed wire all around us, but the wire in Vught was not electrified. Near the entrance, the German officers' staff quarters, a long building, two stories high. Through the middle, an arched doorway and in front an enormous parade ground, the *Appellplatz* (the roll-call ground). How often did we stand there, waiting to be selected, sent to Auschwitz to the Final Solution! In rain, shine, heat, and bitter cold, or just marching goosestep around the damn place. And all around the camp the evenly spaced watch towers with their revolving searchlights and lonely occupants.

We were herded into barrack no. 26C, huge in appearance from the outside and even larger once we were inside. Bunk beds, three high, row upon row, in the "bedroom." We were assigned beds. The "dining room" was outfitted with long benches and tables. Easy to get used to accommodation. Not so, however, the "bathroom"—six hoppers on either side facing each other without any partition. It was quite a challenge and took some time before one got used to it. Perhaps it was its crudeness that prompted the German guards, male and female alike, to shun it. And, in due time, perhaps because of that, the "bathroom" became a kind of social gathering spot, cozy and safe.

We must have been a motley crew those first few months in Vught, old and young, German Jews who had fled their homeland and taken refuge in the Netherlands, and, of course, Dutch Jews. There was a *Männerlager* (men's camp) and a *Frauenlager* (women's camp). One barrack in the latter was turned into a children's camp.

Shortly after our arrival, while passing by it, I saw again the three children of our coworker from Hirsch, their faces pressed against the windowpane. The beautiful long hair had been coarsely sheared off the girls' heads, almost to the scalp, and those big black eyes were now even bigger, peering terrified out of those scared, drawn little faces. Those eyes will haunt me for the rest of my life. There were at least 300 children in that barrack, maybe even 400, and each day some seven women were randomly picked out of the 3,000 of us to take care of the youngsters. Once in a while their mothers were allowed to visit them.

Barrack no. 26C, which I and my former Hirsch coworkers came to call home, was near the *Männerlager*. Two tall barbed wire-fences separated the two camps. In between them was a narrow road that led to the *Industriehof,* the *Appellplatz,* kitchen, etc. During the early stage of our stay in Vught there were certain days during which husbands were allowed to visit their wives. One young newlywed couple found a vacant bunk on which, oblivious to the world around them and even less to the consequences, they proceeded to make love. It was not a good idea. She became pregnant and consequently was sent to the gas chambers.

The group of men and women that had done *Wehrmachtarbeit* (slave labor for the German military) at Hirsch was put to work at Splitter—one

Wiesje's children looking out of the children's barrack.

of the "factories" in the *Industriehof.* There were also a clothing factory and a very hush-hush operation that we soon found out through our active grapevine, entailed the production of counterfeit foreign currencies and some notorious underworld characters who had been installed there and none of those characters ever left their barracks and apparently had quite the upper hand regarding their treatment.

I became one of the Splitter workers. Before the war, Splitter was a large and prominent fur salon in Den Haag (The Hague). Its furs were elegant and expensive and were worn by members of both sexes of the well-heeled Dutch high society. The entire Splitter fur operation had been transplanted to Vught by the Nazis. The Splitter family—five lovely people—were running the Vught setup, now, of course, for quite a different clientele from what they were used to in Den Haag. We performed the same work here as we had done at Hirsch, making fur coats, hats, and linings for the Wehrmacht on the Russian front. Before being sent to Vught, the Splitter family was detained in Westerborg which was the *Durchgangslager* (transit camp) where the young Mrs. Splitter had met my mother who, with an uncanny premonition, had said to her, as Mrs. Splitter later told me, "I think that you will meet my daughter some day." That was the last I heard from my mother.

Vught became our world, the barrack our home and the women in that barrack our family. Our days started very early. We were called out for roll call when it was still pitch dark. Before that, though, we had to make our bunks military style, with square corners and as flat as a slab, not so easy when, with lights out, you cannot see what you're doing, and several elbows, knees, feet, and other body parts of your close, close neighbors are in the way. After that and still preceding the roll call, there was the mad rush to get to the bathroom. Only a lucky few, of course, would make it. By then it was time to line up for food. Each of us had a tin bowl, about eight inches in diameter, which we guarded with our lives—no tin bowl, no food. Each of us got a small piece of bread and some sort of "soup" poured into our bowls. This was both breakfast and lunch.

All this had to go *"eins, zwei, drei—zack, zack,"* or, translated, PDQ, for it was now time for the roll call. Either we had to line up five deep on a small hillside near our barrack, or we had to march to the large *Appellplatz* in front of the officers' building. Whenever the latter was the case, our hearts would sink. This usually meant selection and a transport to Auschwitz. We could always tell when such a transport was impending because, ominously, we were treated to some kind of sweet soup for dinner the night before and our fear started the minute we saw the gort (sweetened oatmeal or some such) instead of the usual unrecognizable soupy stuff or mashed whatever. Since nobody knew who would get the ax this time, we were all terribly tense and scared, and no one slept those nights.

But when, on the other hand, we were lined up close to the barrack, we knew it would be just another routine fun day at camp. How long we had to stand there depended entirely on the good—or more often the bad—mood of the officer of the day. He and two or three female guards would count us several times until they were quite sure that none of us had escaped that night, and they usually made quite a production out of it. After that, it was *links 'rum* (turn left), and we marched off toward the *In-dustriehof.* It took about ten minutes of goose-step marching to reach our work area. That doesn't sound too bad, but have you ever tried to goose-step for more than a minute while singing and carrying a tin bowl half-filled with lunch? As long as that lunch was not too thin and sloppy, it worked more or less. But when we were carrying soup or the almost steady diet of red cabbage, it became quite a juggling act to retain as much as possible of the "nourishment" in our tin bowls. The singing, however, was not always mandatory because only some female guards wanted us to vocalize.

Once inside the Splitter barrack, we faced another problem: In this place with no room for anything, where the 300 of us worked—each with a half-full bowl—we were at a loss as to where to keep the 300 bowls.

Large fur-cutting tables took up the middle of the narrow barrack and against one wall stood twenty fur-sewing machines of which only three were in rather decent condition. The others were wrecks in varying degrees of decay and almost impossible to work with. The Germans were, of course, hardly interested in the condition of those machines. They harassed us—they wanted the work done fast and well.

Near the windows were large tables with benches for the hand sewers and, wherever you looked under the tables, under the benches, in the middle of the narrow passageways between the equipment, there were large boxes filled with all kind of furs. Fur coats, fur jackets, old fur linings, odd pieces of fur—you name it—some donated by patriotic German women, but most seized from doomed Jews.

In the middle of the barrack, dividing it, were two small offices and in front of them was a pot-bellied stove that was never lit. Rounding out the interior design was a large, partitioned off drying room for the cut fur.

And so the problem was where in this overcrowded environment to store our tin bowls that contained our daily food, which provided our only sustenance. Well, there were the window sills, and we soon became adept at erecting an offset wall of tin bowls with food in them. It was an art to stack them on the narrow ledges so they would not topple or tip over. That was merely the beginning. The rest of the bowls were kept under the tables and benches wherever the fur boxes had left some space or were forced to make room.

Bundles of work were distributed, and the place came alive. It was heavy work that had to be completed in record time. But being dead tired, never fully rested and, on top of that, straining under bad light, we really worked against all odds. Around noon we were allowed to eat our "lunch" during a break of five to ten minutes, which was how long it took us just to undo the walls of tin bowls. Then it was back to work until about seven, goose-stepping back to the *Appellplatz*, waiting there to be counted, counted again and recounted some more—it seemed to take forever—then back into the barrack, where a tiny piece of bread awaited each of us, and finally dropping dead into bed.

Chapter 3

Vught

Once in Vught, and for some time thereafter, we continued to wear our own clothes, whatever we happened to have on when nabbed by the Gestapo, and we could send out of the camp letters, always censored, and receive mail, also censored. We were even allowed to receive packages during those early days in Vught. But when letters and packages suddenly stopped arriving, we knew why. The few Jewish relatives and friends who had managed so far to elude the ever-tightening Nazi manhunt and even managed to get some stuff together to send to us in the camp, were finally captured and also sent off.

Trains kept arriving at Vught almost every day, disgorging young and old, tired and bedraggled. There were weekly "selections" for transports to Auschwitz. The German officers and capos who accompanied the transports to Auschwitz, were only too happy, upon their return, to tell us every last and gruesome detail of the activities there. We didn't want to believe them in the beginning, but slowly we realized that these were not tall tales or stories to scare us but rather the awful reality that faced each of us sooner or later. In the face of the certainty that death was so close, life became very dear, and yet there was the wish that it all would end and be over.

Our camp was very crowded at that time. Not all prisoners were working in factories. Some worked in the camp itself, in the kitchen or in the *Effektenkammer,* a storeroom filled with clothing confiscated from Jews, and many others just marked time, trying to be as invisible as possible and keeping out of the way of the green and black uniforms. Most of the factory workers, whether from the Splitter or the clothing shop, were young people. They had been rounded up and brought to Vught with their parents, who were too old, and then sisters and brothers, who were too young to work in the factories in the camp. We felt lucky to be the right age, but most of us had a family member or a close friend in the camp who was not needed for work and therefore was prime material to be selected by the insatiable horror machine. Each of us lived in fear of the transports—a fear not for oneself but for the ones we loved

In our barrack was a young and pretty girl, younger than most of the Hirsch workers at Splitter. Her name was Lore. Blond, blue-eyed, tall and slim, she was brought to Vught with her parents, and her father had been sent in one of the first transports to Auschwitz. Lore became a worker in the clothing factory. Her mother was judged too old to work. Then one day the rumors that preceded every transport started again: "Everybody this time" . . . "Only the old" . . . "Only the young" . . . Lore's mother couldn't take it any more. That morning she was found hanging from an overhead beam in the rear of the barrack. Somehow she had fashioned a noose out of some material. Then I thought that she was too weak and had given up too readily. Now I look at that suicide in another light. I feel that she was very strong, very resolute to take her fate into her own hands.

Lore became one of us, one of our little "family," the younger sister of each of us, and we all loved her. It took a long time for her to come to terms with a deep-seated sense of guilt that she had survived but her mother had not. Or so we thought. She had come to terms with it. But many, many years later, after she had been liberated and had lived for years in America where she married twice and had a daughter, she too took her life. Perhaps she had inherited a tendency to depression. It sometimes runs in families. We'll never know.

Every week there were tragedies, so many of them profound and awful that it would take a lifetime or two to recount them all. But, as I noted before, we, the workers, were the lucky ones. We went to work early in the morning and came back to the barracks late at night, too exhausted to care very much.

Our commandant at that time was a tall, ramrod straight man with aloof, icy-cold eyes, whom I can still see vividly in front of me without even having to close my eyes. But I don't remember his name, perhaps because, he was so remote and never dealt with us directly. The man who did deal directly, and was responsible for us, the Splitter group, was also tall but heavyset and I doubt I'll ever forget his name, Reinecke. His rank was *Obersturmbannführer*, and he had a deep rumbling voice, and more importantly and fortunately for us, an earthy sense of humor. On more than one occasion he shut one or even both his eyes to some irregularity. I would still love to know his inner thoughts of Hitler, the Nazi movement, and, in particular, the role that he himself played in this drama.

He patrolled the *Industriehof* on a bicycle. He left us pretty much alone, and when he barked out an order or punished us, usually by letting us stand "in formation" for a while, for whatever great misdeed we had perpetrated, we could always detect a twinkle in his eyes There was just one thing that, for some reason, he could not and would not tolerate and that was our wall of tin bowls on the window sills. But there simply were no other places where we could stack and keep our food rations unless we ate it all in one sitting and then stacked the bowls inside each other and go without nourishment for the rest of the day. It posed a predicament that had to be dealt with.

We posted a guard. As soon as Reinecke was spotted, there would be a "first alert." When he got off his bicycle, the situation became critical, and the lookout would yell "Elijah!" (the name of one of our great prophets). We would all race to our tin bowls, get them off the window sills, and into the fur-filled boxes. (I never got used to eating hairy cabbage.) One day our lookout goofed, and Reinecke walked unexpectedly into the shop. He looked around a bit astonished, called out, "Elijah!" and

Reinecke waiting for us to remove our tin bowls.

disappeared. After we recovered from the shock, we got the bowls off the sills as fast as we could, and when Reinecke walked into the shop the second time, having given us enough time to hide them, he inspected the premises and left with a big grin on his face. He really was quite a character.

There were more sinister characters. One was a mean and sadistic *Scharführer* (squad leader, a noncom rank) nicknamed "Bochel," hunchback in Dutch, which is what he was. His concept of compensating for his relatively low rank and his good Nazism was by demonstrating sadism, how much pain and suffering he could inflict, which we were spared at the outset of our stay in Vught but were to taste later.

Another was the SS officer who usually took the roll call. A young man with blond hair, blue eyes, and a *Schmiss* (a dueling scar across his cheek), he walked around with a little whip under his arm, a mean smirk on his face and one of many *Aufseherinnen* (female guards), idolizing him, by his side. His favorite was Annie, a blond and beautiful girl who was very proud of having become recently impregnated by him. One *Aufseherin* I remember well was Susie who, with black hairy warts on her chin, looked like a witch and was one of the nastiest females I had ever encountered.

The boss of this elite group of *Aufseherinnen* was a rather nice, elderly, and high-ranking female officer who in the pre-Nazi time had been a teacher at an all-girl high school. We saw her only during our first few months in Vught at mail call. We saw, of course, many more German officers and uniformed personnel than mentioned here—the camp was crawling with them—but the turnover was enormous, and we prudently steered away from them as much as possible.

The camp police, capos, were another elite group selected by the Germans from the criminal prisoners of the camp; they ranged from common prisoners, thieves, bank robbers, and rapists to murderers and thugs and whatever else a society felt compelled to do without. For example, there were Erich, a killer and bank robber with half of his nose and one ear blown off in a shootout with the Dutch police long before the outbreak of the war, and his pal Piet, a small and ugly safecracker of worldwide renown. The capos were supposed to keep the rest of us in line.

They and other former residents of a Dutch high security prison had been brought to Vught and housed in a separate barrack. They took their responsibilities seriously as our duly appointed capos. They terrorized and brutalized us all to a degree often exceeding the Nazis themselves. We hated them no less than we hated our German captors.

Life in the concentration camp Vught had settled into a routine. Those who did not work in the factories made themselves as useful as possible in the barracks. There was the kitchen detail headed by Rosje and Saantje, two Dutch women in their midtwenties. Another detail cleaned the barracks. A group of older women was brought daily to the *Industriehof* to clean there. In that time we also acquired a camp elder, a spokeswoman

Our Aufseherin, Susie.

named Bertel. She was highly capable, strong, and tall, and had a twelve-year-old daughter with her. Completing the group of important individuals in our *Frauenlager* were a female physician, Dr. Levy, and the dentist, Dr. Leuwenbach.

A similar group existed in the *Männerlager*. The camp elder there was a Mr. Lehman, whom I had known in Amsterdam before the war and

whose daughter, Marianne, was a teenaged friend of mine sent to a concentration camp on the first transport from Amsterdam The male camp was attended to by a doctor who was usually stationed in the *Industriehof*. One day a flea made itself at home on the particularly sensitive bodily part of the poor dear physician. It was, of course, nothing particularly unusual in a concentration camp. But it was the spot where the flea had settled that was a bit vexing to him. To get rid of the nuisance, the doctor stepped into a broom closet, dropped his pants and started hunting the lightfooted insect. At that very moment, one of the elderly ladies, wanting to put her broom in the closet, opened it, saw the doctor in all his masculine glory and happily called out, "I haven't seen it in years, it still looks the same—'*helemaal blouw!*' [all blue]." I suspect this may have been one of the last happy moments in her life.

It was summer by now and a very warm one at

"Helemaal Blouw!"

that. The work with the fur in the stifling barrack was grueling and just to make sure we would have no strength left to escape, we were given a second job, cutting beans for a cannery. Thus, we were dead tired at night and looked forward to the luxury of sleeping the few hours we were permitted. But at this point, the window warfare was full blown. One half of the bedroom occupants, mostly the German Jews, wanted the windows open for the *"frische Luft"* (the fresh air), while the other half, mostly the Dutch, wanted the windows closed. Maybe they liked the *"warme Mief,"* the warm, nasty smell. This went on and on. Nobody got much sleep, and everybody was at each other's throat until we had nocturnal visitors from across the two tall barbed wire fences. The window warfare was over. The windows, understandably, stayed open.

Neither those barbed wire fences nor any others in Vught were electrified. Instead, the Germans had fastened cowbells here and there on the wires so that they would ring out a warning as soon as somebody touched the wire. Now, as I noted earlier, close to the fence in the *Männerlager* was the barrack housing the capos, and it was no challenge for them to render the cowbells useless. They didn't remove them nor in any way alter their exterior appearance. They just took out those little hammers and thereby the last obstacle to fairly unimpeded nightly visits. To this day I don't know who all the "lucky" damsels were who hosted the rendezvous, but since a number of them contracted syphilis or some other nasty disease, the secret couldn't be kept sealed.

Erich the bank robber with half as nose and only one ear, was one of the visitors of the night. He and I shared a mutual hatred of each other that could have cost me my life, but more about that later. To Saantje from the kitchen detail he must have been Prince Charming. Or, perhaps, she needed a man, any man. And at night, in the dark, who notices noses?

There was just one more challenge awaiting the "suitors" once they were over the fence and inside the huge barrack: How to find among 300 the right bed occupied by the anxious sweetheart. The solution lay in the counting: second row, fifteen beds down, third bunk up. Easy!

But the best laid plans of mice and men. . . Annie, our proudly pregnant female guard, had a favorite sport. She would suddenly reassign beds, usually just before bedtime. At this point we still had some earthly possessions consisting of extra clothes, books, trinkets, etc., some of which were stored at the rear of the barrack but most of which were stashed under our straw mattresses. The relocation meant schlepping those possessions to another bed located at the other side of the barrack, bumping into others busy moving, losing half of the things, trying to find one's new bunk, sometimes ending up two or three in the same one and, in general, making a big mess of the entire undertaking.

Annie would be running around, hair and cape flying, yelling and screaming and making things worse if that was possible. It was always late at night by the time we were more or less settled in our reassigned bunks. Of course, during this whole maneuver there would be no time nor, indeed, any chance to warn the lovers from across the fence and even less to convey to them the new countdown of beds. Saantje's bunk was thus taken over once by a sweet old lady, and no one will ever know who was more surprised that night, Erich or she!

Deprived of family and friends, the women and girls occupying the same barrack did their best to compensate for them. Inside the large "family group," smaller groups formed. One group would become very jealous of another, and it would be considered almost an act of treason if a member of one family made friends with members of another. We became quite clannish, and I am afraid that I was guilty of such "treason" because even though my "family" didn't like it, I had friends in many of the other groups.

My "family" consisted mostly of girls who had worked for Hirsch in Amsterdam but now and then, here and there, a few "outside" girls would be admitted to the group because we liked them, had the same background, or just became a part of us by sleeping in the bunk on top or below one of us. There was, of course, Lore whom we had "adopted" after her mother's tragic death, and then there was Inge who never felt that she belonged to the group. She became my personal friend. Inge had many problems that she could not resolve, not then and not later. But the two of us liked each other, played the "piano" together on the wooden tables—our favorite was a Haydn sonata for four hands—and now, so many years later, we are still friends.

We all tried to keep our spirits up against a backdrop of fear, of not knowing whether we would be still alive next week or even tomorrow. We were in a limbo. Our parents and families and friends were taken away from us. Each of us alone and stripped of individual identity. Our backgrounds, our station in life, rich or poor, did not matter. Nothing mattered any more. All the props were gone. The only things that were of importance were one's own standards, one's strength, and how much one was willing to give of oneself and how good a friend one proved to be.

Chapter 4

Many Deaths and a Tiny Satisfaction

Every two weeks or so there was a "selection" for the transport to Auschwitz. The Dutch quotas for the crematoria had to be filled. On "selection" day we had our roll call on the large *Appellplatz*. We lined up, hundreds of us, at arms' length from each other. In the deathly silence you could hear the slow steps of the Germans row up and row down. We didn't dare move. We hardly dared breathe. We knew all too well what was happening. We didn't have to look. Every so often a finger would be pointed at someone, the sign to get out of the line and go over to the other side of the *Appellplatz*. Slowly, agonizingly, with Prussian precision, one by one enough individuals were "selected" to fill the quota.

You could feel your blood drain and your heart pound with each step of the German entourage approaching you. The terror grew to an unbearable level as you waited for the finger to point at you. And when it didn't, you felt like a death-row inmate, already strapped in the electric chair to be executed for a crime you didn't commit, getting a last-minute reprieve. You were spared this time. The end for you was not yet, not this time.

During those horrible hours, and it took hours, I tried to concentrate on the rising sun, the clouds in the sky sailing far, far away from this place, and I tried to let my thoughts sail with them. I tried to recall Mark Twain's travels on the Mississippi River just to get mentally out of this hell. It was not easy especially when a finger had been pointed at a friend or someone standing next to me. Thus, slowly, the camp was thinning out.

By now, the Jews picked up in Holland were sent directly to Auschwitz without first stopping in Vught or in Westerborg. Also by now, a group of about 100 women, Dutch non-Jews, were marched into the camp and into a special security compound. Our grapevine once again had no problem even with the special security and we learned that these women were Underground fighters. An agent provocateur had managed to infiltrate the Underground and betrayed a large group of it. The men in this group had been sent directly to Dachau and the women were brought here, to Vught. We saw them sitting on the ground behind the double barbed wire fence. They seemed different from us. There was no fear or anxiety on their faces. Rather, their faces, eyes, and demeanor expressed such defiance and courage as to make us ashamed for lacking them. But, within a few days, while walking past their compound we found it empty. It took a few more days for the tragic truth to reach us. Our commandant had forced them all into a small windowless room with a downward sloping floor—for easier cleaning—and locked them inside where they suffocated.

Our despair and sense of utter helplessness in the face of this horror defy description. There was, however, a man who was not helpless and who took it upon himself to react. He was the German doctor, a member of the staff, a man of small physical size but of enormous guts. He somehow had the commandant arrested and executed although I have no idea to this day of how he managed it or what pull he had in Berlin. How ever he managed it, I try to console myself with a hope that it was a retribution for the suffering agony of those brave women of the Dutch Underground resistance.

By now we were totally cut off from the rest of the world. Heretofore we heard from the new, almost daily arrivals about what was happening in the war, not that it was encouraging. The Nazis were winning all over and the Allies apparently had either given up or were simply unable to turn the tide. It was all quite discouraging, and the only bright light amid this gloom were the nocturnal and more and more frequent air raids.

Whatever mail we once were allowed to receive had now stopped. Only the Red Cross was permitted to deliver necessities, among which were sanitary napkins which we no longer needed because we had stopped menstruating. Concurrently and mysteriously, the Red Cross saw fit to send us the biggest imaginable barrel of mustard. It's possible that the Red Cross felt that we were in need of some kind of uplift, and mustard seemed the right medicine for empty stomachs.

Somehow the enormous barrel was deposited inside the Splitter barrack and, once opened, it exuded the smell of mustard that was intolerably awful. So, with a lot of pushing, pulling, and swearing, we moved the barrel outside, in front of the shop. The mustard, I must admit, gave the red cabbage a certain snap. The only problem was that poor Inge became addicted to the mustard.

The air raids originating across the Channel were now not only nocturnal but also daytime events. Not that any bombs were dropped on us, but whenever an Allied plane was spotted, the alarm sounded, and if at work, we had to leave the shop. We would run, clutch our precious tin bowls, get out of the barrack, and line up in front of it. If there was some logic to this, it eluded me. I could not figure out why we had to get out of the barrack. Either the Germans felt that we were safer outside or that the barrack was safer without us inside. The only beneficial effect of this exercise was to give Inge an opportunity to sneak up to the mustard barrel and get a lick or two of the (to her) heavenly stuff. But, alas, even the biggest barrel will get empty sooner or later. And so did this one. But necessity is the mother of invention and Inge managed to tip over the barrel, crawl inside it, and scrape off the sides and bottom as much as possible.

Inge enjoying the last of the mustard.

The brave Germans were terrified of air raids and they tended to watch the sky more keenly than us and thus Inge managed to get away with it. With mustard now all over her, she had no trouble keeping her friends at arm's length.

During the period when the camp had no commandant, Reinecke did not take advantage of either the situation or of us. His basic attitude remained the same. But not so with the youthful *Untersturmführer,* the one with blond hair, blue eyes, and the *Schmiss,* who felt that now was his chance to show what a good SS officer could and should be like. He started with the morning roll call. Instead of getting up at six in the morning, it was now five and the nastier the weather the longer we had to stand or goose-step around the *Appellplatz* and the screaming, shouting, and punishments were endless.

The soil in the Vught camp was mostly red clay. When it rained, which was often, our feet would sink into the red mud up to and above ankles. On one such morning we had been standing for quite a while in the rain, and we were, of course, soaked thoroughly as we waited for the young SS officer with the *Schmiss* to take roll call.

Next to me stood Floortje, the camp clown. She could talk without moving her lips and the worse the situation, the funnier her comments. I usually tried to stay as far away from her as possible not because I didn't like her—on the contrary, I loved her—but I laugh easily, and it's still hard for me to this day to recall her and keep a straight face. And even the faintest smile during the roll call could mean bunker or Auschwitz. Anyway, there we stood in the pelting rain, dripping wet, our wretched clothes further disintegrating and clinging to our shrunken bodies. We felt and looked like skinny wet rats. Finally, our bigshot officer appeared, as usual straight as a ramrod and, as was his habit, impeccably dressed in his immaculate uniform for the roll call. With him were Annie, quite pregnant by now, Susie and a few other lesser personalities. For some reason today, of all days, he wanted to show off.

As he approached our column he started to goosestep. But one shiny boot got stuck in the deep water-soaked clay, and he fell forward, still ramrod straight, plump into the red mess right in front of me and Floortje. For a second nobody moved. It all looked like a film in slow motion. To avoid laughing I tried to think of all the horror around me while pinching myself as hard as I could. Then Annie screamed, and two of the guards jumped forward to pull the fallen hero out of the muck which had by now gotten a good grip on him. Finally, his entourage pulled him out with a juicy squishing sound and got him upright. The SS officer was barely recognizable. His face, hands, and the entire front of his uniform were covered with a thick red goo.

As usual, someone had to be blamed and, of course, we were it. We spent, therefore, the rest of the day standing at attention. By day's end we had sunk to our calves in the muck but the vivid memory of that same muck nearly swallowing up the SS officer made it nevertheless a happy day for us.

Around that time we acquired a new commandant. Things went on as usual for a while, with us in the work commandos leaving in the morning and returning at night dead tired. The weekly transports to Auschwitz continued, and the barrack and kitchen detail had shrunk to a handful of people. We had all lost a great deal of weight and started to look like the concentration camp inmates pictured in the by now familiar photos, film reels, and documentaries.

Chapter 5

End of Children, Philips

One night we had an unexpected roll call on the *Appellplatz*. No rumor had preceded it nor did we get the sweet "gort" the preceding night. The commandant himself showed up for the inspection and selection. He started slowly up and down the rows looking at a fiercely frightened bunch of females. We could feel that something unusual was about to occur and not knowing what to expect made it so much worse. He began to point, one, two, four, ten. About twenty girls were picked out. I was one of them. We were told to remain while everybody else was ordered to march back into the barracks.

It was the beginning of one of the worst nights in my life. We were told that the children's barrack in the *Frauenlager* was being closed and its occupants were to be sent to Auschwitz. What we had feared and never dared to talk about was now at hand. The twenty of us were commandeered into that barrack.

The children, most of them asleep two or three to a bunk, were awakened with screams. Their frightened eyes looked at us. None of them uttered a sound. They had long since learned that crying brought only punishment. We were told to get together the few belongings that were still theirs and pack them into boxes or knapsacks. Even though I wanted to say something to those tiny scared faces looking out from the bunks, wanted to hold them and stroke them, wanted to rip this nightmare to shreds, I couldn't for fear of breaking down and crying and risking making things worse.

In silence, for all of us were choked up, we packed. Little torn clothes, old ravaged dolls, a few much read children's books. It didn't take long, this packing. There wasn't much. The stuff was sent to the German children "from the grateful Dutch population."

While this was going on in the children's barrack, the *Aufseherinnen* went from one barrack to the other announcing that the children would be transported out of the camp the next day and offering the mothers a choice: To go with their children or to remain in the camp. Most chose the obvious—they went with their children. But some had other children hiding underground somewhere in the Netherlands or had concluded that since they could not help their kids by going along with them, they should try to stay alive in the

28

hope of being reunited with their husbands by some miracle some day.

That night will always haunt me.

What these mothers were forced to experience was nothing less than to choose between two hells. That experience became my anguish over and over again in recurring nightmares. In those years we learned to live with the deaths of children. We saw hundreds of little shoes and huge piles of clothes that had belonged to youngsters. We were together with mothers whose children had been shot in front of their eyes. But this drama in Vught, the drama of that night belonged to all of us. These children had become our children, and with their death a part of us died.

Soon after the children's transport the clothing shop was closed. Again we were assembled on the large *Appellplatz*. The Splitter workers were told to move to one side so that only the workers from the clothing shop and the clean-up and kitchen detail remained. When the selection began we were surprised to see the finger pointing at the tall and beautiful girls and at a couple from the kitchen detail. The others were marched out of the camp to the end of their existence.

The tall and beautiful women, twenty to thirty of them, were separated from us and moved into one of the many now empty barracks, one that was also known by the fancy name of *Effektenkammer*, store room. Our grapevine had broken down somewhere along the line, and we had no way of knowing what was happening behind the walls of that particular barrack. Four days later, two women of that group stumbled out and over to where we stood for roll call. They had red and swollen eyes and were crying. They joined us without any explanation, and we never asked for one. They were the only ones. The other girls had disappeared and the *Effektenkammer* barrack was empty again. How these two tall and beautiful women managed to escape whatever horror and brutality they and the others had been subjected to was a mystery to us and was never cleared up. What did become apparent was that Herta, one of the two, was now able to get away with pretty much anything she wanted and, as time passed, she became our enemy, siding with the Nazis. Eventually, after our liberation at the end of the war, she was prosecuted. But that was far into the future which, at this point, none of us believed we would live to see.

Now, nearly half a century later, I know that those other beautiful girls were sent to Treblinka for macabre experiments. They were medical, physical, biological, reproductive, and endurance experiments. They included surgeries of the most depraved nature designed to test incredibly bizarre hypotheses. Only one survived.

The weather finally got warmer and our German captors began to worry about our health. To prevent any insects from carrying any sickness into the barracks, it was decided to fumigate them. Cans of Blausäure-Zyklon B (a Prussic acid derivative) were brought into the camp and distributed among the barracks which, of course, fueled rumors that we were going to be gassed right there in our own barracks in Vught. Soon enough, with those cans in front of the still inhabited barracks, the entire camp population was called out to the *Appellplatz* and a large transport of men was selected.

Among them were the Meisners: Paul—still in his twenties and the youngest, most handsome and pleasant—his father and brothers, all fine and well-known furriers. Paul was bright and a delight to be with, and he was the only one to be pulled out from the transport by the Splitters and allowed to remain in Vught for the time being.

Four days later we were ordered to evacuate the barracks earlier than usual and without roll call marched to the *Industriehof.* Our barracks were gassed that day, and when we returned that evening, we learned to our utter horror that Paul Meisner had somehow never made it out of the barrack. Maybe he had been so exhausted, as we all were, that he never heard the command to get out, and it was still too dark for anyone to see him in the bunk. Or, again, the explanation might have been even simpler: His allotted time had run out. He died the same day that his father and brothers did in the crematoria, which it took them and the men of the transport four days to reach. Paul would have been on that transport if the Splitters hadn't saved him.

Vught's population shrank considerably. Summer turned into autumn but otherwise time seemed to stand still. It began to dawn on us that the "other side," England and America, couldn't or wouldn't invade and rescue us. The hopelessness grew steadily deeper and the motto "try to win time" was turning into a bad joke when suddenly, one night, after only about an hour of sleep, the barrack doors were flung open and Annie, Susie, and some other *Aufseherinnen* started to scream at us. Initially we didn't understand what was going on or what they were yelling since it was so unexpected and fast. We were, of course, frightened even more than normal but, finally, we understood those bitches and witches. We were to pick up everything that we still owned and possessed and bring it with us to the *Appellplatz.*

Carrying little bundles, all our worldly possessions, we stumbled out into a dark and chilly night. Prisoners were coming from all directions carrying stuff, losing much of it, bumping into each other. We were shouted at and pushed toward the *Appellplatz* and the entire camp was in an uproar. Normally things went with Prussian precision but not tonight. Large wagons with wooden wheels and planks on both sides, no doubt to be horse-drawn but minus the animals, were standing ready, and we were ordered to throw our bundles onto them. Next, we stood in formation as usual and were ordered to undress down to our panties or underpants as the case might be. Our shed clothes were added to the wagons' contents while we shivered in the cold night with no idea as to what all this was about. Wildest speculations were being whispered from one to the next: We would be shot on the spot; we would be marched out to dig our graves, etc.

We stood on that wide open field for what seemed for ever while the wagons containing our clothes and belongings were pulled and pushed past us and toward the officers' building. The last links with our former selves were thus stripped away and carried off.

We were finally marched into a barrack inside which capos and guards, male and female, stood behind tables laden with huge piles of striped prisoner garb. As we shuffled past the .ables a piece of clothing would be flung at us. If you were a man, you also were thrown a cap. Females got blue handkerchiefs with white stripes and polka dots. Nothing exemplified better the proverbial Nazi penchant for order and precision than the fact that in the dark the smallest "dresses" were thrown to the biggest girls and vice versa. It took quite some exchanging of those blue and white prisoner sacks among us before everybody had a "garment" that more or less fitted. Also along the line we were giv n a piece of tape with a number printed on it and, of course, the yellow *Judenstern* (Jewish star) without which we would have felt naked by now. Thus, when we returned to the *Appellplatz* attired in the blue and white striped prisoner uniforms with kerchiefs on our heads, we felt and looked the part of K.Z.ers, the German abbreviation for *Konzentrationslager*—inmates of concentration camps.

When we marched back to our barrack, it was already getting lighter with the approach of the morning and as we entered what had become our "home," we turned speechless. The entire place had been ransacked and turned inside out and upside down. The stuff we had kept on shelves and in boxes at the rear of the barrack was all gone. The mattresses had been pulled off our bunks, and many ripped open. Straw was strewn everywhere. The bunks, usually in neat rows, were now all over the place. Here and there, among the straw and half empty mattresses were remnants of our former "wealth," a page out of a book, a forlorn sock, a handkerchief. I presumed that they were looking for valuables but we were too tired, too exhausted to care. We just stood there, dumbfounded, and stared. Not for long, though. Somebody, probably Susie or Annie, screamed at us to clean up, to stuff the straw back into the mattresses and to sew the numbers and stars onto our outfits. *"Schnell! Schnell! Macht schnell!* [Hurry up! Hurry up! Get a move on!]"

This was easier shouted than done. First of all, without lights and still before morning's daylight, everybody was getting into everybody else's way trying to push the straw into those unwieldy and limp bags. Then, once we had accomplished that, real difficulties started with trying to sew up the lumpy mattresses and attach the numbers and stars on our "uniforms." Even if each and every one of us had been issued a needle

Getting our "beds" ship-shape.

and thread, it would still have required more time than what was allotted. But with only a few needles to sew up 300 mattresses, numbers and stars to be sewn on same number of uniforms, the task proved to be impossible, and therefore we were punished. I don't recall what the punishment was but, most likely it was the usual: no food for a day or two or goose-stepping around the *Appellplatz* for hours.

Yet another flurry of rumors swirled around. Splitter would be closed and all of us sent to Auschwitz. Having learned that there was almost always some truth to rumors, Auschwitz and the gas chambers seemed very close. Then one day a tall, good-looking gentleman in civilian clothes showed up. He spoke Dutch and introduced himself as an executive of Philips, the largest electronics and radio manufacturer in the Netherlands. He told us that Philips was planning to open a factory in Vught and anyone under thirty and single could apply for work. Come, he said, in the next few days to a designated barrack for tests. Tests for dexterity, intelligence, eyesight, and I forget what else.

Almost everybody of that age group grabbed this opportunity. We sensed, instinctively, that Splitter's days were numbered and that any work for Philips would by now be more important for the Third Reich than making fur coats. It took a few days for the tests to be administered and none of us had any way of telling how well or badly we had done on them. We knew nothing, and the weeks that followed during which we learned nothing were increasingly filled with anxiety born out of uncertainty. This, in turn, gave rise to the feeling, which grew daily, that the entire project for some unknown reason must have been abandoned.

On a cold, rainy, and miserable November morning we were marched onto the *Appellplatz*. We had little doubt that this was it, that this time we would all form one huge last transport to Auschwitz and the crematoria. Again we were standing there at arm's length from each other waiting. But instead of the expected and familiar "selection process," with German officers walking up and down the rows, pointing a finger, names were now called out alphabetically from a list. It was unusual, strange, and, as always when something unusual or strange happened, we were scared. Those whose names had been called had to step out of the formation and line up on the other side of the *Appellplatz*. At this point we had, of course, no idea what awaited either group, the ones called out or the ones on the opposite side.

One of my best friends, Hetty Hecht, was standing next to me. The last name starting with G was called out. Now came our turn, the H's. Hetty's name was not called. Then I heard my name, "Hellendag Eva," and I knew that Hetty and I were separated and I lost, a wonderful friend. But I had not known then that she refused to take the Philips tests. Just before the outbreak of the war she had married a young man who was a diabetic. Theirs was only a civilian wedding and not one under a chuppa, as part of a religious ceremony. Their marriage had never been consummated. Hetty knew that Philips would reject her husband, and she did not want to be accepted without him. I often think of her and still miss her.

There was also a set of twins with their mother, all three small, very thin and with tiny features. Somehow all three had managed to stay together and now there loomed the threat of separation as only the names of the twins were called out. But somehow they managed to get their mother from one side of the *Appellplatz* to the other. How they did it and how they got away with it remains a mystery to me.

The last name on the alphabetically arranged list was Lotte's, our tallest friend. When it was called out, she joined us while the list was neatly folded, and the group of officers walked away leaving us standing, soaked, shivering in the drizzle and trying not to think. We were a small and sad group. Then came a command: Our group was to fall into our usual column of five abreast, turn left, march off, and proceed toward the *Industriehof.* We had passed the Philips tests. We were chosen to remain alive to do some work beneficial to the Nazi cause.

The other group went the way of so many before it, taken to Auschwitz where death came not from gas chambers this time but from typhus. One solitary friend managed to escape from there and the epidemic and we found each other, much later, in an outside work detail of Auschwitz in the *Sportschule.*

As we entered the Splitter barrack in the *Industriehof,* I broke down and wept at the sight of Hetty's empty place. It was the only time I ever cried in the camps. A good friend came over and held me even as his eyes were also overflowing with tears. Whatever it was that we did during the next few days was insignificant because all the members of the Splitter family and most of their furriers were gone by now, and we realized that within a few more days this particular chapter of our life in the concentration camp would come to an end. In the meantime, though, we—mostly young girls together with some "older women,"—were moved together into a couple of barracks. Among us were Bertel, our *Lagerälteste* (the camp elder), our doctor, dentist, and a few others who had somehow managed to hold on to Vught. But, most important for us, the reason we were chosen to remain here was that one of our fellow inmates was Dr. Kohn, the famous physicist, whose renown reached through some powerful connections into the highest echelon in Berlin. We never ascertained who those connections were, and inevitably there were rumors. But she was one of those rare women who never shared with us any details of her private life. She kept her own affairs strictly that, her own. Dr. Kohn was an immensely bright, quick, and courageous woman of small and stocky stature, with light blue and penetrating eyes, exuding strength. She became our mentor, guide, and teacher, and we were her students. The realization that our survival depended on how well we learned under her tutelage turned us into her eager and dedicated disciples.

Sure enough, the Splitter shop finally closed its doors and a few days later we began to work in the Philips Barrack. At first, the work was quite bewildering. Some of us were assigned to small machines mounted on tables with a box containing parts and tools including a jeweler's magnifying glass. Someone told us that we were to put together small radio sending tubes called P.500, which were miniature pentodes. To do that we needed a loupe, a jeweler's magnifying glass, to see the parts to be assembled, parts barely visible to the naked eye. First, of course, we had to learn how to put the loupe into one's eye socket and then to keep it there. The P.500 had to be flawless.

Other groups were put to work assembling different parts of some electronic gear. Initially we had no idea what we were doing except for a vague notion that all those parts were for radio transmission, which was important to our captors. It was obviously imperative for us to be as indispensable to the Third Reich as possible. Accordingly, Dr. Kohn gave us lectures secretly at night, and the bathroom became our lecture hall, where she made sure that we were always at least a step ahead of what was required of us by the Germans.

Life in the Vught concentration camp had changed. Only a small group of us remained while the number of guards and capos stayed the same, which meant there were more of them to watch and harass our small number. We were puppets dancing to the shouts and whistles of capos and guards for whom it was a game, the object of which was to see how much they could make us dance. For a while even rumors of transports ceased and our world had become isolated and suspended. Fortunately for us, our work was genuinely important and every aspect of it continued under the watchful eyes of the Philips people, which insured a kind of check and balance. We saw less of Reinecke but more of the sadistic Bochel who was happiest when spying the slightest irregularity and quick in dealing out severe punishment. Naturally, we were all terribly frightened at the very sight of him.

Also changed was the food and the way it was served. One barrack in the *Industriehof* was designated as "dining barrack." Large pails of food, consisting most often of thick mashed potatoes with some peas or beans stirred in and without the slightest hint of any kind of taste, were brought in during our now extended lunch period. The change was in quantity. The food, in fact, was perfectly awful. Roosje and Saantje again headed the kitchen detail and dealt out the portions which were generous enough and would have satisfied the hungriest mouth if they had been edible. But to leave any kind of food in our tin bowls would have been one of the worst offenses, on a par with pregnancy.

It soon became obvious that Saantje was pregnant, and no one doubted who the father was—none other than the hideous and earless Erich. I cannot understand to this day how any female could have let him within arm's length, much less make love to him. But, for whatever special favors she got out of it, and Erich was certainly able to dispense them, Saantje's pregnancy proved fatal. As soon as a German officer noticed it, she was sent to Auschwitz and the gas chamber. Erich became our "dining room" capo, and we had the distinct "pleasure" of seeing him daily. I hated him. Once he sat opposite me at a table and his mere presence made it difficult for me to swallow the pasty and tasteless junk. He started to scream at me, "*Fress, oder ich schlag Dir eine ins Fressbrett bist Du blau bist!* [Wolf down or I'll slap your snout till you turn blue!]"

At that point I just had enough. I got up and in a barely controllable but quiet fury snarled back at him, "*Halt dein Maul!* [Shut your trap!]" and the entire dining room was so quiet that you could have heard a pin drop. My reaction could have cost me my life, but an astonished Erich got up, left the barrack, and from then on kept his distance from me.

As soon as we became familiar with our work for Philips, the tempo increased. There was apparently an urgent need for those components, and in due time some of us, who made fewer mistakes than others, were promoted to controllers, and I was one of those. The promotion meant that now I was not only responsible for my own mistakes but also for those of a group of others. A mistake could very easily be interpreted as sabotage and mistakes were easy to come by when we were all so overworked and tired. We worked seven days a week, twelve hours a day.

Meanwhile, the canneries around Vught now needed their seasonally harvested vegetables cleaned and cut. That chore was assigned to us in addition to our work for Philips. Thus, for weeks, we sat at night with mountains of beans in front of us, pulling the "hairs" off and slicing them.

We were so exhausted that we turned into giddy zombies. Respite arrived when the weather turned cold and the bean supply finally ran out. But until then, during our bean processing period, we were so tired and our backs ached so much that I can't imagine how we could have been efficient workers. The commandant, leather gloves clutched in his palms, with his entourage respectfully behind him, came to inspect our progress with the beans every so often. Why? I don't know. Maybe he and they had nothing better to do.

The weather turned nasty, cold, and wet, and we were thoroughly chilled. Then one day we found a huge pile of old and dirty coats in the middle of the *Industriehof.* "*Los. . . schnell!* [Pick one, fast!]" we were ordered. It sounded easy enough but the ensuing scramble turned into a rag-picking contest. Everyone tried to get at that pile at the same time hoping to pull out as warm a coat as possible but in the process sometime two or three of us found ourselves tugging at the same coat each of which was a man's garment. It must have tickled our "protectors"' sense of the perverse that these coats had once belonged to men who were of no further use to the Third Reich. I finally ended up with an old and very threadbare coat that was much too long and that made me feel and probably look like

Scrambling at the pile of old and dirty coats.

an old, old man. One sleeve was torn and there wasn't a single button to be found on it. And yet, when, after the winter during which that wretched coat did not keep me very warm, I had to give it up, I felt quite sad. The coat and I had become close friends and we had shared some moments that one could not forget so easily.

The air raids had ceased almost completely, and we felt hopeless and crushed by a growing fear that the world was forgetting what was happening and turning its back on us. There was a radio station in the *Industriehof* that transmitted German news and German music most of the time. Operating the station was Jaapje Peters, a young Dutch Christian prisoner. He once managed to let a few of us listen to Beethoven's 9th Symphony, the Choral. The glorious singing of Schiller's "Ode to Joy," which is the final movement of the symphony, that we heard here in the camp, was simply unbelievable in context. I still can't listen to the 9th today without feeling a huge lump in my throat and being transported back to Vught. But, most of the time, the radio played old *Schlager* (hits) from German movies or Germanic *Helden* (hero) music performed by the Nazi marching bands. In between, there was, of course, the "good news" from all the fronts assaulting us constantly. Since it went on and on, we got used to it, blessedly, and even immune to it. And when it started to blare out some Christmas carols, we realized sadly that another year was ending and that the coming New Year of 1944 didn't look any more promising from where we sat than the previous one.

We decided, nonetheless, to stage a New Year's "party." After all, we reasoned, what worse can happen to you if you already sit in a concentration camp? Two of our funniest women composed the most marvelous song, a few of us staged some kind of a suspense drama and the whole thing was a huge success, mostly due to the German big and little shots being all much too drunk to care what we were doing. And then winter turned into spring and the woods surrounding Vught began to smell wonderful. Here and there we could see a tree in bloom, white or pink against the dark background of bare trees. Being in a concentration camp was now even more unbearable.

Chapter 6

Auschwitz-Birkenau

Great excitement filled the air one day as the Germans, from the top brass to the lowliest, displayed a bad case of the jitters. The only one among them to maintain more or less his cool was the sadistic hunchback Bochel, who seemed to be bemused by it all.

One night we were officially told what we had already heard through the grapevine, that *"grosser Besuch"* (big shots) were expected. Our regular work, for once, took a back seat. We were all turned into a cleaning crew. Pails, brooms, soap, and even rags were handed out. The first thing the female half of the cleaning crew managed to do was to help the rags disappear. They were, after all, much more useful as patches for our rapidly and constantly disintegrating clothing or as material for socks, underpants, and a thousand other vital items. After that, we all began to clean with vengeance. It was a change from the routine, and there was nothing we could do but obey the screamed and menacing orders. There was no method to the cleaning frenzy. Some guards would run in, shout an order, and run out, and before we'd start to follow that latest *Befehl* (order), another guard would appear and bark out a different command. The ensuing pandemonium was quite funny. There was water everywhere, brooms were flying, tables and benches were soapy and soaked. Even windows were washed with rags shared by our fellow male prisoners. After three days of this comical bedlam, the camp was shining, and everybody was in a state of nervous shock, everybody except the Bochel. He had had himself a great time at the height of the cleaning frenzy emptying pails of dirty water over scrubbing females and poking them with broom handles.

Throughout this period we tried to find out who was this *grosser Besuch* but to no avail, and I doubt that any of the guards knew either. Finally, the big day arrived. We went early to work in our spic-and-span Philips barrack. Our guards and capos were stationed in every corner, all nervous. I can still feel myself sitting in front of my machine hearing the heels clicking and the sound of many pairs of boots striking hard against the cement floor of the barrack. And there, with a large entourage, was none other than Heinrich Himmler, the head of the SS and, in power, second only to Hitler. Now we understood the jitters and began to feel them quite strongly ourselves. The "great man," obviously on an inspection tour, walked slowly down the aisle, asking questions, examining tubes and other parts, somehow conveying the sense that he really knew what he was looking at and that he better find everything without a blemish. He proceeded to the front of the room where a few officials, both from the camp and from Philips were gathered to welcome him. Among them was Dr. Kohn. The commandant introduced the gentlemen from Philips, some camp bigshots, and then, "*Und das ist Frau Dr. Kohn.* [And this is Mrs. Dr. Kohn.]" Himmler extended his hand to shake hers

The Bochel's "fun" in the cleaning frenzy.

but with her hands clasped behind her, she shook her head and said, *"Ich glaube kaum das Sie meine Hand schütteln wollen, ich will bestimmt nicht Ihre schütteln.* [I don't think you'd want to shake my hand, I certainly don't intend to shake yours.]"

Himmler just stood there staring. It was now as quiet as a tomb. No one moved a muscle. We barely breathed. We were sure that this was our death sentence. I know that the blood drained out of my head, and I had to use all my will power not to faint. I guess we were all waiting for some order to get out, line up, or whatever. But, instead, Himmler turned on his heel and without another word left the Philips shop with his entourage behind at his heels.

Thoroughly shaken up, we were sure we hadn't heard the end of this incident, and while awaiting Himmler's revenge, we tried to behave and work as normal as possible. But nothing followed. It was as if the episode had never happened.

Besides Himmler we had a number of other visitors in the period we worked at Philips, high-ranking Germans in and out of uniform, Dutch officials, representatives from other Nazi-occupied countries, all evidently interested in what we were doing. Dr. Kohn was, after all, a pioneer in miniaturization of electronic components, and the equipment we operated was clearly as new and vital as the components we were producing. Dr. Kohn kept us, of course, as always, a jump ahead of the Nazi scientists so that we could answer most if not all the questions they put to us.

Toward the end of our shift one day, we had some high-ranking uniformed visitors, and as the hour came for us to march back to our barrack and the roll call, they and our commandant walked ahead of us. They were in no particular hurry strolling along, arguing a little and even stopping now and then. The trouble was that we were marching goose-step fashion right behind them. I was in the second row and in front of me, close behind the high and mighty visitors, was Lotte whose legs were so long that her knees were at a level where most of our legs began. If she had stretched out her legs in a full-blown goose-step, she would have kicked the slow moving high uniforms right in the ass with her every step. But Lotte, having learned how to cope with both major and minor crises, came up with a new version of the goose-step: After smartly bringing up her knees to her stomach, she would rotate her feet a few times as if stirring something in a pot. Thus she stayed in step, the visitors' buttocks were out of danger, and I almost exploded trying not to burst out laughing. Finally the military brass turned off and we proceeded to our roll call.

Winter was ending, days were growing longer and warmer, and someone decided that we no longer needed our coats, which thereupon were confiscated. Then, upon entering the Philips barrack one day, we were startled by the sight of the Bochel sitting on a crate, motionless, staring straight ahead as if into another world, completely oblivious to us. The hunchback's silence and detachment from everything around him was so strange, so out of the ordinary that it frightened us. After a while he got up and walked out without uttering a word or noticing anyone. He was not the same Bochel who would punish us severely for any minor infraction such as sneezing or coughing or have us stand for hours when he would decide that he didn't like the way we goose-stepped.

We had no ideas nor could we even guess the reasons for this drastic change, and, as usual, rumors abounded. Finally, Erich, the half-nosed and one-eared bank robber, came out with the reason for the change in the Bochel's behavior: Each of his four sons, all apparently tall and handsome young men, had been killed within a short span of time on the fronts of the Third Reich. Their father was broken. Soon thereafter we were shipped out of the Vught concentration camp and the Bochel had tears in his eyes and kept repeating, "*Gott beschütz Euch!* [God help you!]"

But before we were dispatched, more rumors circulated. Philips would be closed or taken over by the Dutch workers. We would be transported to Poland. Both proved accurate. Men were the first to go. The roll call was longer than usual on that hot day, and when it was finally over, only the women were allowed to leave the increasingly desolate *Appellplatz* while the men remained there for three days and nights without food or water waiting for the train to take them to Dachau, a destination kept secret from all of us and only revealed later. We tended to take it for granted that Auschwitz was our final destination.

Then one evening, we were served "gort," the sweet soup, and we knew that our turn was next. The following day we were marched to the *Appellplatz* and from there, in a long column of five abreast, to the tiny railroad station of Vught. We boarded a long, long train that waited for us, consisting of countless cattle cars. We had all our belongings with us: our striped dress, polka-dotted kerchiefs, and our tin bowls. We were traveling light. And just as well. The train was not pulled into the station itself where we might have entered the cars from the platform but was parked on tracks away from the platform. None of us had ever realized how very high above the ground those cattle cars were. It took some agility, long legs and arms to "board," and the screaming and yelling of the officers and guards did not help any, and for once there wasn't much they could do about it. Those among us with the longest legs and arms, with a push from the ground, got in first and then pulled up the next ones who were given a boost by those still on the ground. The last to board had to be the lightest since there was nobody left to give the needed push.

With practice in the years to follow, we became experts at that maneuver but this being our first time it took some doing, and it lasted much too long for the officers and guards. At the end of it there'd be about fifty of us in each cattle car and later even seventy and then more than 100 would be pushed into a single cattle car. Some thirty years later, when I again saw those cars, I was stunned by their small size and could not understand how fifty of us could ever get into one of them, let alone 100.

After we were more or less "settled" in our car, the *Scheisskübel*, the shit-pail, was shoved aboard, one per car, a common household pail that could not hold very much, and then the doors were slid closed. Except for some straw on the floor, there was nothing else. We sat on the straw on the floor and waited for the train to move. There was really nothing else we could do. Someone tried to start us singing one of our camp songs, of which we had quite a few, but nobody felt much like it. After a few feeble attempts the hesitant singing ceased. We sat motionless waiting through the night, a strange, dark, eerie, and very silent night. The train never moved an inch.

It was dawn when the doors were pushed open, and we were ordered out of the cars. We could only guess since no one ever told us whether this was just a dry run or, maybe through the efforts of Philips, the order to ship us out had been reversed. But we marched back to the camp and into the *Industriehof* in a manner of "going home." It turned out to be a short-lived "homecoming."

Four weeks later, June 2 and a beautiful morning, we were marched again to the railroad station and ordered into cattle cars of a waiting train. As soon as we had all "boarded" the train, it started to roll and gather speed. It was for real this time.

A cattle car—let me tell you—is hardly a comfortable mode of transportation, and I do not recommend it to any one. The *Scheisskübel* soon proved wholly inadequate. The moment it was half full, the constant swaying motion of the train would keep it that way, half full. The "contents" slopped and sloshed out of it. The straw, the floor, our clothes and our very bodies were drenched, and the stench became almost unbearable.

The boards of the cattle car walls were not fitted too well together, resulting in cracks here and there through which we could peer outside.

Once in a while the train would stop and we could read the names of the stations, *Hannover, Halberstadt . . .* and we knew we were going east. Twice or three times the doors were opened, the pail emptied, and everyone received a tiny piece of bread. The German towns and villages that our train passed did not look at all war-torn. They looked intact. Apparently nothing happened there, no bombs, no damages. This depressed us deeply. We had no doubt, just from the names of the cities our train encountered—Dresden, Halle, Leipzig—that we were on our way to Auschwitz. And we were equally sure that these were the last days of our lives. But even so, the sight of a Germany so unharmed, so beautiful, made us really mad. After four days and nights we crossed into Poland and came through Katowitz (now Katowice).

The very thought of Katowitz can still drive me into a deep depression. We passed rows upon rows of the dirtiest houses I had ever seen. Women in clothes as black as their faces and hands, searched along the tracks for pieces of coal, which they gathered in baskets or their aprons or just carried in their hands. The city looked as if it had been bombed centuries ago, been forgotten and never rebuilt, a sight I'll never forget. Yet I couldn't take my eye off "my" crack between the boards. Then came woods and meadows, beautiful tall dark trees until we approached another station. More tracks came into sight, switches, lights, and trains and trains and more trains, all cattle cars—Auschwitz-Birkenau. We had arrived. It was June 6, my mother's birthday and I didn't know it then but I was near her ashes.

Nobody, but nobody who has ever been in one of those cattle cars on those railroad tracks running in front of Auschwitz and looked through the cracks toward that camp can imagine the horrible sensation. If you were not there yourself, you cannot grasp what it was.

Yes, I know there are hundreds of books about it, films and television shows produced about it, lectures given and pilgrimages made there, and I will not try to describe here my feelings or thoughts of that moment for the simple reason that I cannot. I would have liked to but I don't know how to describe pure fear, horror, and, worst of all, the feeling of complete helplessness.

We arrived there in the afternoon and remained locked inside the cars for what seemed an eternity. We didn't know it then, but there was a reason for the wait. We had to wait our turn. Train after train was arriving filled with human cargo, unloaded crudely, and herded past many different uniforms on the platform, and past Dr. Josef Mengele, who kept pointing to the right but mostly to the left. It took hours.

We could see the darkening sky painted red by the glow of flames spewing out of tall chimneys while a horrible odor penetrated everything and mingled with the stench inside our cattle cars. We didn't talk. It was deadly quiet in that dark box on wheels. Finally, the doors were slid open, and we were screamed at and ordered out. It was drizzling and the sky was dark except for the tongues of fire trying to lick it.

The camp itself was illuminated by glaring white lights fastened on the poles of the electrified fence. Electric wires gleamed and seemed to stretch forever as did the gray rows of barracks. We stood on what has since become the most infamous train station platform in the world and listened to orders barked at us but which we did not understand. Then we marched on and through the iron-grilled gate bearing an equally infamous slogan: *"Arbeit macht frei.* [Work makes you free]." I was not particularly aware of the gate at the time nor did the officers congregating around it make much of an impression on me. Also, unknown to us, Dr. Mengele and his adjutants had been alerted to our special status as a *Sonder Kommando,* a special detail, making us, for the time being, immune to his finger of death. We marched past him unaware of his significance.

We marched down a long, dark, narrow, and slippery road with the gleaming electric wires on one side and the gray barracks on the other. We had no idea where the road was leading, whether to the barrack or to the dreaded *Brausebad* [shower bath], that entrance to hell that we knew so much about by now. All of us were numb and tired. I don't think any of us had any emotions left. We felt totally dejected. The road took us past barracks that were like ghosts in the bright light, their empty windows like eye sockets in a skull.

We reached our quarters, barrack No. 13. I remember it because someone asked whether this was a lucky or unlucky number and I answered that since we were Jews, it was a lucky one. We lined up in front of the ugly, long and gray building and faced the opposite one. And there, in those windows, those empty dark holes in the wall, were faces staring at us.

Faces of human beings, yes, but at first we weren't even sure whether they were faces of living or dead, men or women. The heads were clean shaven. There were no expressions in those faces nor any movement. Just large dark eyes staring, matching the staring "eye" of the barrack. We stood there, in a fine drizzle, for a very long time and when we were finally allowed to enter our new "home," we were soaked and icy cold even though it was June. Once inside, we did not believe our eyes. Now,

Our vis à vis in Auschwitz.

after so many years, the interior of those barracks has become familiar. But to us then, it looked horrifying.

I'll try to describe briefly the barrack the way I remember it, without the superimposed images of photos and films so widely shown since then. Nothing could be drearier, dirtier and more depressing than this place. The long low building was cut in half by a low, three-foot-high gray concrete wall. Pushed against the outer walls and the glassless windows were three-tier high "shelves" that were bare, about six feet wide and deep and hewn together out of rough wood. The empty windows gave the drizzle free rein to soak those shelves that happened to be pushed against them.

Once again we waited, this time standing against the three-foot-high wall—the Selection Wall as we came to call it. And we waited dutifully until, at last, an *Aufseherin* entered along with our Polish "stubova," the camp abbreviation for *"Stubenälteste,"* a girl or woman in charge of a "room" in the barrack. Eta, our stubova, was a rather pretty girl, Polish-Jewish, who had already managed to survive three years here at Auschwitz, a fact we had no way of knowing at that time. Two other girls joined her. One, Lubova, was the stubova of the other end of the barrack while the second turned out to be the "blockova," in charge of the entire barrack and thereby the boss of both Eta and Lubova. And all three were Polish-Jewish, tough, and showing not the slightest trace of emotion or, indeed, humanity.

In the true form of the place and occasion, we were shouted and screamed at. It went on for a good while, even though we had no idea what it was all about. Then a few of us were grabbed and unceremoniously shoved onto those shelves. It took no time for us to grasp the general idea: These were now our beds, six to a bed, the lucky ones on the lower, the less lucky had to climb and be pulled up to the second and third tiers. Even with our emaciated bodies it was still quite a feat to fit six of us onto one of those shelves. We all lay down on our side, on the same side, with our knees fitting into each other's, like spoons in a drawer, and I am sure that sardines in a can were comfortable by comparison.

Once we had lain down, we had to remain motionless, and we encountered an unexpected and painful problem. In those cattle cars, the rhythm of the uncushioned wheels rolling over the clefts in the rails had immunized us against any need for a motionless and silent bed. But now our "beds" were fixed, and to lie still on one's side for any length of time was pure torture, but if one of the six turned, the other five had to turn also. It took many sleepless nights to get rid of the cattle car hangover and to get used to our new beds and bed companions. That first night, in the drizzle, we also had to decide whether to get our heads or feet wet. The consensus of our "bed" was for wet feet. And, of course, we still had on our wet "garments" since they were all we had. There was no place to put them to dry out, no mattress, no blanket, just the wooden shelves and the drizzle.

We were hardly bedded down when the wake-up whistle blew. It was 3 A.M. and time to get up. It was still pitch dark outside and still drizzling. And just like in Vught, we again had to line up outside and in front of our barrack, five deep. The bald-headed girls—they were girls—from the opposite barrack were also lining up and even though it was still too dark to get a good look at them, we recognized them as the huge dark eyes that were staring at us upon our arrival the previous night. Now the place was eerily quiet except for the Germans and the capos shouting and the muted shuffle of hundreds of feet accompanied from somewhere by the sound of a drum being beaten to a macabre rhythm. Hanging over it all and permeating everything was the overwhelming stench from the chimneys of the crematoria, a hellish omnipresence.

Male and female guards came by, counting, walking back and forth, again and again. Slowly, oh so slowly, it became dawn. We were finally able really to see the girls on the opposite side. We were deeply shocked by what we saw and did not realize that very soon we would look like them.

After what seemed like interminable waiting—wait for what?—there was some stirring at one end of the long column. It was the arrival of the *Scheisskübel*. Imagine a contraption like a miniature hay wagon with a huge wooden kind of a washtub on top, being pulled by two girls and pushed by two more, the four of them in gray prison garb and black aprons which identified them as somewhat of an elite.

Some commands were shouted. We did not understand them but our vis-à-vis did. By fives they walked up to the wagon, clambered up, pulled their "dresses" up, sat on the rim of the tub and did what everybody sooner or later had to do. After a few moments, another command, those first five got up and off the wagon, and it was the turn for the next five.

It was all yet another unbelievable spectacle, and I remember wondering what would happen once the tub was full and soon enough I found out. About one fourth down the line a command was barked and five of those ghostlike girls somehow got the thing off the wagon and schlepped it away while another tub was brought in, placed on the wagon and thus carried on a brisk business. When that column was finished it was our barrack's turn. The wagon finally reached the line of the five of us. In front of me was my friend Elli whom I had known since Koblenz, but I don't remember who the other three were. In any case, the five of us had just finished a very private function very publicly, the *Kübel* was about three-quarters full, and we were ordered to get it off the wagon and dump its contents *auf dem Abfallhof,* (into the dump). There were five handles conveniently attached around the rim and despite the weight, which was more than we had expected, we managed slowly to drag the stinking thing

The Scheisskübel

toward its destination. The task took all of our meager strength, and we would have succeeded had Elli's foot not got stuck in the mud. Our precarious balance was upset and she got a good dose of the *Klosbrühe* (contents) over herself and the girl in front of her.

This was the only time, I believe, that we were really grateful for the rain which had by now intensified and was pelting us. At least some of the muck was thus washed off those two, and Elli was, after all, my bed companion. I must admit it was a bit selfish of me, but. . . When we returned at last with our empty *Scheisskübel*, the wagon had moved pretty far down the line doing its brisk and precisely timed business.

Soon, another vehicle came into view on the opposite side. It came to be known as the *Fresskübel*. You might call it our version of the meals-on-wheels. There was one bowl ladled full of some slop and passed down the row. You were allowed three gulps and then had to pass it along. It tasted awful but by now we would have eaten *anything*. . . .

It was daylight now and the *Aussenkommandos* (workers who did not labor in the camp itself) were going off to their work. The drum started up again and in the distance we could see long columns marching away from the camp. The girls from the barrack across from us also marched off while we remained still standing. I don't remember how long we stood there or who gave an order or what it was, but we did start marching away from our barrack toward a huge, gray, and terribly ugly building. It was the *Brausebad.* Somewhere across a door was a sign, "*Eine Laus Ist Dein Tod* [One louse is your death]." Remarkably ironic in view of the large rats scurrying freely all over the floor. We undressed. By and by we were herded into a shower hall with about twenty genuine shower heads on the ceiling out of which came, lo and behold, a trickle of water. We were ordered to get washed. There must have been some 400 of us, naked women, trying to wash ourselves under those heads that dispensed a mere trickle of water. It was a generally futile effort, and we didn't even try. Our biggest concern was not to step on or be bitten by those rats.

After a long time, and they gave us plenty of it together with little water, we were told to get into the drying room. This contained wooden benches in long, climbing rows. We were told to sit down and get dry. Not being wet, we could only comply with the first order. We sat down. Then one by one we were called out. We did not know what awaited us next and therefore were scared and expected the worst. I was certainly no braver than anyone else, and suspect that my legs were shaking just like the rest. But the moment I crossed to the other side of the door, my first impulse was to laugh.

I was in some kind of a barber shop and there, before me, stood my nude fellow prisoners—at least I thought that these were the same girls I had shared my life with for the past year or so. But now they were all bald. I never realized how vital hair was to one's appearance, even ugly, dirty, stringy hair. My best friends, now without their hair, had become barely recognizable. I had no time to scrutinize their faces, because I was pushed into a barber's chair myself, and a rather nasty Polish girl, also a prisoner, started to shave my head. I didn't care so much about being deprived of my hair as I did about my head feeling cold.

Elli followed me into the barber shop, and I could see that she didn't quite recognize me. I grinned at her, and I knew she had a hard time trying not to laugh. The shearing of our heads took a long time and turned us into caricatures of ourselves. We were very quiet, very tired, very hungry, and very cold. We were next given different prison garb, ordered to dress, and herded into an adjoining room where, at small tables, sat a bunch of girls, again Polish Jewish inmates, with long needles, inkwells, and large ledgers. We were told to form a line and as we came alongside the tables one of the girls would grasp our left arm, tattoo a number and a small triangle on it and push us forward. The girl who tattooed my arm pushed me while still holding the needle in her hand. It caught my right pinkie and left on it a tiny bluish mark. The triangle identified us as "workers," a most sought-after identification. My number was 78-364.

All numbers were, naturally, carefully marked and registered in large ledgers. Once numbered, marked, and registered, we were marched out of the building and it was only then that many of us, perhaps all of us, were finally convinced that this had indeed been a genuine shower and not the gas chambers. It was now time for the toilet. Even though we had gotten used to shocks and tended to expect them, we were startled when we entered this facility. Long, long wooden slabs ran down the room, two in the middle and one on either side along the walls. Cut out in those wooden slabs were holes, close to one another, 150 of them in each row. Ergo, there were 600 "potties" in this ladies' "powder room." We formed four columns and marched down the two lanes between the inner and the outer "potties" until the first of us reached the end of the line. Then, on command, we had to sit down, do what one does while sitting on a toilet seat whether one needed to or not, get up on the command whether ready or not, and march out of the building. There was, as usual, no toilet paper or any other item of luxury, and we neither expected it nor were used to it anymore. It was getting dark, and from far away we heard the sound of a drumbeat. The *Aussenkommandos* were returning "home."

Our first day in Auschwitz drew to a close. I must admit that it had not been a boring one, not for a minute. We were marched back to our barrack and made to stand on roll call. The *Scheisskübel* came again, and then everyone got a tiny piece of a very dark bread, about one square inch in size, and finally we were allowed into the barrack and onto the shelves to sleep.

It seemed that as soon as we had fallen asleep at last it was 3 A.M. already and time to get up to begin another fun day in Auschwitz. The truth, however, was that it was all so horrible that I tried to think myself out of this place, to make believe that another Eva, or only my body, was here, that I myself, my mind, my soul, my very being was somewhere else. I tried to think of my childhood, my parents, books that I loved and music. But, for whatever reason, this mental escape which had worked in Vught, did not work here. Maybe it was the constant stench surrounding us, the fear that was in the air, as thick as an all-enveloping blanket, and the absolute conviction that this was going to be the end of the line.

The few times that I succeeded in spiritually leaving this hell, I usually ended up with my thoughts in Amsterdam the first day of the war, the beginning of my journey to this inferno.

Chapter 7

1940

It was a beautiful, bright, and blue-skied day in May—May 10, 1940, to be exact. I awoke and, as I always did, turned the radio on only to hear that the Netherlands had just been invaded by the Germans. I got up and looked out the window. The beautiful, blue Dutch sky was dotted with hundreds, no, thousands of white spots. I woke up my mother and together we watched in pure horror as those small white spots grew bigger and bigger and became parachutes with soldiers, German soldiers, attached to them. Some landed in our garden behind our building, some we saw landing on the roofs of the houses opposite us, on the garage roof in the rear of the garden, on the street, everywhere.

My grandmother woke up and joined us. The radio was still on, and we listened to the news of the war. The Dutch had thought that they had a foolproof secure defense system, namely, to flood the dikes. The Netherlands is crisscrossed throughout with them and the idea was to open the floodgates, whereupon all the low-lying areas would be submerged, rendering them impassable to German tanks. The Dutch population felt secure with this arrangement. What it did not know at the time, of course, was that a fifth column of German "moles" had infiltrated every level of the Dutch military as well as its civilian government.

Five days later the war was over. The Germans were victorious. The defeated Dutch population stood grimly watching as one German military vehicle after another rolled down their cobblestone streets.

For us, who had fled Nazi Germany, hoping to be safe in the Netherlands, this was a terrible blow. We knew what was coming and what to expect. Anyone who could fled by boat to Sweden, England, or wherever a boat would take them, or across the Belgian border to France, Spain, Portugal, and eventually to North or South America. But the world seemed loath to open its doors. There were not many escape hatches, and the few that were required a great deal of money.

Many went underground. Anybody with connections and enough cash tried to disappear. And I want to say on behalf of the Dutch that many Jews were saved by the sturdy heroism of the general population. But far too many had no way out and were trapped, knowing that sooner or later the efficient German machinery—designed and organized to free the world of the "undesirables"—would catch up with

52

them. We—my mother, my grandmother, and I—were among the latter group.

It all got under way quite innocently. Everybody had to register: name, address, age, and of course religion. The purpose, as explained at that point, was to enable the authorities to hand out food and clothing stamps in an orderly fashion, in which everyone was given an identification card with a photograph. Jews had a prominent *J* printed on theirs. Also, to make sure that every Jew knew that he/she was a Jew, he/she got an additional name: Sarah for women, Israel for men. A little later, Jews had to wear the notorious yellow star with the word *JOOD* (Jew) printed on it in imitation Hebrew letters.

The next steps to rid the world of the "Jewish menace" came in rapid succession. Curfew at 8 P.M. No Jews allowed in stores, movies, theaters, any public buildings, or schools. It was the last that was devastating for me. I was in the last year of school, about to graduate, and now, again, I had to leave what I saw as my future and my friends behind. However, a decent Dutch school administrator let me take my examinations early and granted me my diploma.

The first time I was forced to leave school—at the age of thirteen and one year after my father had died—was in Germany, of course, when no Jewish kids were allowed any longer in any but Jewish schools. Then, the last two years in *Hilda Gymnasium* were not easy either. The two Jewish kids in my class, Helga Treidel and I, had to sit in the last row, were not allowed to raise our hands and were called *die Unkräuter* (the weeds). Both of us were shunned by our classmates, and if they talked to us at all, it was only to call us names or to spit in our direction. They used to be our friends and playmates. They were all children of upper class parents. It was at that point that my mother sent me to our relatives in the Netherlands where I resumed attending school only to be thrown out shortly after the German invasion on that May 10, 1940. But the difference—and an enormous one it was—was that my Dutch friends remained my friends up to this day.

But now, out of school, the big question was what to do. At that time, I had a good friend, a furrier, who thought it prudent to teach me his trade which, as I indicated in previous chapters, had saved my life thus far. Soon the *Aufrufe* (summonses) started to come. The Jewish teen-agers were called up to serve in "work camps." Initially we tried to believe it, perhaps because it was easier and less frightening to believe than to admit one's secret fears. I received my summons at the same time that 499 other Jewish youngsters, all between seventeen and twenty-three years old, got theirs. We had to assemble in a school yard, the 5th H.B.S., Hoger Burger School, a senior high school. It was a bright, cool but sunny morning and we milled around, talking a bit but mostly we were silent and apprehensive.

Finally, the German officer who was going to process us arrived with his entourage. A card table was set up, a chair behind it, and another long table with neat rows of papers, our papers, on it. The fun could now begin! And as always, true to German form, our names were being called out neatly in alphabetical order. It all took a very long time, but then we had nothing better to do anyway. It got hot as the day progressed, and there was no shade in that schoolyard. Then came my turn: Hellendag, Eva. As I stepped forward, I noticed that the two front legs of the card table were slowly moving inward and would collapse sooner or later. They were probably tired, too. I started to giggle, seeing in my mind's eye the whole shebang landing on the ground, and that giggle saved my life.

The officer looked up and yelled at me, *"Was lachst Du so blöde? Hier ist nichts zu lachen!* [What are you laughing at so stupidly? There's nothing to laugh at here!]" He pointed to the heavy entrance door to the school and ordered me to stand behind it until he was good and ready to deal with me. There was nothing else I could do but obey his command, and so I went to stand behind that blessed—and I mean blessed—door, and I stood there all day long. At one moment, I recall, I was in extreme need of a toilet but that's about all I remember of that long, long day.

Evening was approaching, and it was getting dark, and the last of the youngsters were processed and pushed into one of the waiting trucks which, once full, started immediately to roll out of the yard. I held my breath, too scared to move or even to think. The card table, the legs of which had withstood the signing of 500 death warrants, was folded up along with the chair and the long table and put into a truck, which left the yard together with several cars carrying off the officer and his henchmen. I had been forgotten and left behind the door.

I couldn't believe my luck and dared not leave my corner behind that door. But it was now really dark, and as I tried to consider my next move, I heard voices and steps. I froze. The voices were Dutch and female, and since the footsteps entered the school building, I surmised that these were the cleaning ladies. I mustered just enough courage to enter the building very carefully. One of them was starting to clean the long hall. I could not see the others, but I heard them. I walked up to the woman who had just put her mop into a bucket of water. She was big and had a hard face, and I was already afraid that I had made a mistake. But I could not back out. I told her of my plight and never saw a face change so fast. Her features softened and tears welled in her eyes as she pulled me quickly into a small room, not much bigger than a closet. She called some of her coworkers, and together they transformed me into a passable cleaning lady, replete with a broom, mop, and pail. I worked alongside these wonderful women that night and into the early dawn and then walked out of the school in their midst into the streets of Amsterdam.

I wish to take this opportunity to thank those wonderful women and explain why I like to paint pictures of cleaning ladies and make drawings of them over and over again. The 499 other youngsters were never seen or heard from again. Only much later did I learn that the boys were sent to Mauthausen and the girls to Ravensbrück.

Once back on the streets and in daylight, I walked home. My mother was overjoyed to see me, and she hugged me while tears streamed down her face. She had me back, and I was in her arms. Alas, it was only a very short interlude, but one that I'll cherish forever. Now, however, I faced another problem. Officially I no longer existed. I was gone and, for all practical purposes, dead. My

viors, the Dutch cleaning women of the high school.

name had been crossed off the list in my presence by the officer just before he decided to send me behind the door. My identification card with its beautiful *J* printed on it had been collected along with those of the other youngsters when we entered the schoolyard and probably served later on as evidence of the efficiency with which the Netherlands was made *judenrein.* Without an identification card one could not obtain food coupons. Thus I ceased to exist. However, thanks to my friends in the underground I was "issued" both a new ID card and food coupons.

Soon afterward, workplaces were created for Jews with skills useful for the Nazi war efforts, and I, as a furrier, was one of those. My friend who had taught me that skill proved to be right. I was put to work at Hirsch and Co., which, as I pointed out previously, had been a large and very elegant department store. The lower two floors had been converted into offices for the Nazi machinery while the top floor became a kind of a preconcentration camp until the real one, Vught, would be finished and ready. Now we were making fur coats, fur linings, and fur hats for the Wehrmacht, the German army.

Also at this time razzias, roundups, began with a vengeance and escalated into nightly dragnets not only in Amsterdam but throughout the Netherlands. The German as well as the Dutch Nazis went from house to house routing out the Jewish population and probing in non-Jewish homes for Jews who might have been hiding there. The three of us— Grandmother, Mother and I—knew, of course, that sooner or later it would be our turn to be dragged out of our home. In anticipation of that I had for some weeks been removing our valuables from our apartment and taking them to our non-Jewish friends for safekeeping: our silver, my mother's and grandmother's jewelry, and our photographs, which turned out to be my most precious possession. The most valuable and important to me of these personal possessions was my sewing machine. I took it apart and piece by piece carried it to the house of one of my friends.

It is easy, in hindsight, to judge the relative wisdom of the chances we all took under those circumstances, but we all fervently tried to believe that the whole horror—the war and the Nazi regime—would end soon and life would return to normal. Our hopes were in vain. Much later, I did get back my valuables from two of my friends, but the third one, who worked for the Underground, fell victim to the Nazis. The most important for me were the photos that I managed to save under extreme danger to all of us.

Inevitably our turn came. The doorbell rang in the middle of the night, and there stood two Dutch Nazis, both well known all over Amsterdam and much feared. The three of us were ordered to dress, to take our backpacks that had been packed and ready for weeks and to get out of the apartment. The door was closed, a seal put over the lock, and we were taken to the *Sammelplatz* (assembly place), which happened to be the same school where my giggle had saved my life

Once again our ID cards were checked and collected from those to be sent to Westerborg, the transit camp, or to the concentration camps. Mine had a large *W* stamped on it, which meant that I was a worker for the Third Reich. I was pushed to the left, my mother and grandmother to the right. Mother smiled bravely at me and waved. It was the last time I saw her, and to this day, I still see her as she was then: She was wearing a large black felt hat, and she smiled at me.

I was taken into the school's gymnasium, and the only other person there was a young woman in labor. The door was locked behind me. I had never in my life felt so alone and so helpless as at that moment. I instinctively knew that I had lost my mother, but I also knew that I had no time now to think of that or of myself. Somehow I had to help this woman deliver her child. At first I banged on the door and yelled for a doctor or nurse. But I soon realized that neither would materialize and that I was IT. I took a deep breath and tried to remember what I knew of childbirth. The young woman, Leentje, was in a terrible pain and screamed. Then I remembered Pearl Buck's *The Good Earth.* I had read it several times, thank goodness, and with my memory of that book as my guide, I helped deliver a healthy baby. I held the infant in my hands and wondered what to do next when the door opened, and somebody entered. I don't remember too much of the next few minutes, because I must have passed out. When I came to, I was alone in the gym. It was eerily quiet all night, and at daybreak I was called out and sent on my way to work.

Eventually I learned that the mother and child were well. They had been whisked away by a Dutch nurse and hidden first in one of Amsterdam's hospitals and then somewhere on a farm. Both survived the war. Meanwhile, though, I was again in a dilemma: Where was I going to stay?

Slowly but surely the Jews had been rounded up into a ghetto in the few square blocks in the *oude Zuid* (the old South), of Amsterdam. There remained a few Jewish families living here and there in their homes or apartments. Some of my family members were still in their old home. So, when I finished work, I went to their house.

One family member worked for the Underground. She was the most beautiful woman with blond hair and shining blue eyes. With such looks she felt secure. She had not lived in Amsterdam before and did not think that anybody would know who she was. She walked around the city without a star and after curfew and would bring false papers and messages to and from members of the Underground. But someone did recognize her. She was betrayed, and two days after I had moved in with my family, the entire household was picked up. I did not know what happened to other family members. I was put in a prison in *Einzelhaft* (solitary confinement). The Nazis thought that I too was working for the Underground. I was dragged out of my cell at all hours of the night and day and brought before some officers, who asked endless questions until I could no longer remember even my birth date. Again and again the same questions, with whom did I work, who were my connections, where were the hiding places, on and on and on.

I became quite disoriented in that small, dark cell. I felt I would go mad without somebody to talk to. And then I heard a faint banging. I don't remember what day or night it was. The banging seemed to be coming over one of the pipes running along the wall of my cell. At first I didn't pay much attention to the rhythm of the sound but suddenly I realized that it was in the Morse code. I understood it, having learned it before, and, in fact, I was rather proficient in it. I then responded even though I did not know who initiated the coded contact or whether the Nazis were eavesdropping. Some other prisoners joined in and pretty soon we had ourselves a full-fledged banging conversation along the pipes. It wasn't that I or the others revealed much or learned anything but at least I didn't feel so isolated anymore.

On the morning of the fifth day my cell was opened, my coat and shoes were thrown at me, and I was told that I could leave. I remember standing in front of the prison in Amsterdam, a few yards from the school I used to attend, with absolutely no idea where to go. Eventually I realized that the only place I could go to was Hirsch and work. Of course nobody there had any idea of what had happened to me. And I guess that nobody thought that they would see me again. But here I was back with nothing more than the clothes on my back and no place to go after work. A few of my co-workers offered me a place to stay and I gratefully accepted the offer. My friends already lived in the ghetto, and I joined them. I borrowed some clothes, a few odds and ends and a kind of a backpack.

We were allowed to ride the streetcar, though restricted to the front of it, to work early in the morning and return "home" at night followed by curfew. It all ended with one swift and thorough roundup of all of us, the Hirsch workers, and our transportation to and detention in the once magnificent but now only cavernous Schouwburg theater from whence, as you may recall, we were taken to the concentration camp Vught.

Chapter 8

Reichenbach

At this point, try as I may, I ran into a mental wall. I have gone over this in my mind again and again, trying in vain to figure out why there had been no way of escape. It was an exercise in futility, I knew all along, but thoughts cannot be shut off. Not for long, anyway.

Anyway, I did not have the luxury just now to indulge in too much thinking about the past, the present, or the future. It was only the here and now, the dreadful reality of the moment that mattered. Everything had boiled down to simply trying to stay alive, trying not to get sick and then not to get too sick, trying to blend into the gray crowd, getting in and out of the barrack and to whatever work we were assigned.

Looking back now, Auschwitz seems like one long dark corridor full of spider webs, dank and slippery, through which we stumbled with no end in sight. The dramas that were played out around us were horrifyingly incomprehensible, so terrifying that we had to shut our minds against them. The barracks opposite ours had been emptied and filled and then emptied and filled again and again while we killed time with routine. We got up at three in the morning. We stood on roll call, waited for the *Scheisskübel*, waited for the *Fresskübel*, and then waited for the counting which sometime took hours upon hours to be completed. Finally, having been "fed" we would march five abreast on the narrow roads between electric wires toward our work station. As a result of our previous work on radio tubes under Dr. Kohn, we had been designated *Sonderkommando* (special group) and as such we performed mostly busy work. We were unaware of our special status, and this busy work made us very uncomfortable. We knew that whatever we were doing was quite unnecessary, and we were convinced that all we were really doing was waiting for that last march over the *Himmelfahrts Strasse* (Heavenbound street) toward the gas chambers.

I had developed an irresistible urge to touch the electric wire to get it over with. Therefore, my friends never let me walk on the outside of the column. After the long, long day, we marched back to the barrack to stand five deep again waiting for the roll call. Then came the *Scheisskübel* followed by our tiny ration of bread and it was off to bed.

In the beginning of our residence in Auschwitz it rained almost constantly. Our sack garments were never dry. Filthy? Yes. Dry? No. Mine had an additional feature: a red streak down the front. You see, I had been one of the lucky few chosen to paint the barrack floor to impress some high and mighty visitor. The task was both tedious and interesting in as much as the painting—for reasons known only to the Third Reich—was to be accomplished with toothbrushes.

My "artistic endeavor" with a toothbrush in Auschwitz.

We went through quite a number of them. After all, these things were not designed for that purpose. There were about half a dozen of us engaged in this artistic endeavor. Each of us had a box of red Zinnober (cinnabar) stones next to us. We rubbed the stones together until we had in a bucket a little mountain of fine red powder. Actually, we had more of it in our nostrils, ears, on our "dresses" and in the air than in the bucket. The powder in the bucket was mixed with water, and, voila, the paint was ready. According to the stubova who was hovering over me to make sure I did a good job, I must have been doing just fine. I did not understand a single word she said but she actually smiled. And since she did not understand a single word I was saying, I told her smilingly that she was a bitch and that someday I would like to give her a kick in the ass and similar endearments. She evidently liked my smile, and thus I became a great friend of hers—although she was no friend of mine—which is neither here nor there.

My barrackmates were in their bunks watching the six of us paint the floors. They understood, of course, what I was saying, and they never quite forgave me for my performance due to the fact that laughing was a definite no-no. Soon the painting job of going back and forth with a toothbrush across the floor became boring, and if you don't believe me then just try it for four or five hours. I decided to do a little artistic painting. To my utter surprise, my new "friend" was enthralled. I don't remember whether we ever finished that damn floor, but I do remember that every bone in my body hurt.

Life in Auschwitz, if you could call it that, became routine. The everlasting stench never left and never let you forget how very close was death. There is now abundant literature about that place, all true and then some. But there is no way I can find adequate words to depict this hell on earth. There were the gallows, and women and girls were hanged. There was a children's barrack at one time, but the children disappeared. Some of our fellow prisoners were beaten to death or died right in front of our eyes. But let me dwell on "the other side of it all," the human and even funny one.

Mad as it may sound, there was a funny side even in Auschwitz as, for example, the day when the Germans, for whatever reason, wanted to be generous and everybody got, in addition to the daily food allowance consisting of a piece of bread measuring one square inch, a piece of *Harzer Käse,* a cheese from a certain region of Germany. No one who has ever smelled or tasted *Harzer Käse* can possibly imagine the full impact of this "enormous favor!" You can smell the stuff a mile away, and if you want to keep some, even the tiniest piece of it in your refrigerator, you had better pack it in triple layers of the densest material you can find, and even then there's no guarantee of an odor-free refrigerator. On top of this enormous favor we were allowed for once to return to our barracks immediately after our meal. Well, let me tell you something! We had a *Harzer Käse* of tremendous proportion. Just multiply the one inch cube of that cheese by 400. Needless to say, it was quite a cheese and quite a stink! We tried to eat it so we would not suffocate but tasting it was even worse than smelling it. It took us two or three days to get rid of it, and we did it by eating tiny pieces of it at a time. I don't believe we ever really eradicated the smell, and today, the moment I smell *Harzer Käse* I am right back in the middle of our cheese period in Auschwitz.

The work deemed the most appropriate for new arrivals, those "lucky" enough to make it into the camp, was *Strassenbau* (building a street) out of cobble stones, which had to be individually hand-hewn and then pushed into the squashy gray clay. The streets didn't go anywhere, of course, nor did they come from anywhere, but it was a back-breaking work, and the German guards who were in charge of the project screamed and carried on as if the fate of the Third Reich depended on those darn cobbled streets. Oh, well, they probably wanted to show off to get promoted to a higher rank, so they could get away from that hell, and I can't say I blamed them.

Another paradox were the pansies. On the way from one camp to another—say from camp A to camp B or to the kitchen or showers—you passed through gates, which, like the notorious front gate, displayed such lovely maxims as *"Eine Laus Ist Dein Tod* [Even a single louse is your death)" or *"Leben Durch Freiheit* [Freedom means life]," etc. But, next to the gates, on either side, were a few plants of blooming pansies. They looked so sad and forlorn in this wasteland that I actually felt a deep pity for them.

Then one day we were marched toward the shower, following the roll call. I remember the lump in my throat and the butterflies in my stomach because I was sure that we were heading either for the gas chamber or out of the camp and into an *Aussenkommando*. Somehow I had an inkling that we would be bidding good bye to Auschwitz, but I was much too scared to pay attention to that inner voice. We were brought into the same huge room we had entered when we first arrived. But now a rope had been strung across dividing the room into two parts. About half of our group was taken to one side and the remaining half to the other. We had, of course, no idea why we were here, why we were divided by that rope, or worse, who was on the "good" side, if there was a good side, and who was on the "bad" one.

Our little family stood together on one side, all but Elli—she was on the other side of the rope. We were frantic even though we didn't know whether she was on the "good" side and we on the bad one, or whether she would have a chance to get out, or we would. All we wanted was to stay together. Two sisters were also separated, the older one on our side, the younger on the other. When a capo passed by Greetje, the older sister grabbed her arm and begged her to let her be together with her sister. Without uttering a single word, the capo pushed her down under the rope, pulled her over to the other side, grabbed Elli by her arm and kicked her over to where we stood. Elli ducked under the rope, and our "family" was reunited. The capo, all unaware, had performed a double good deed with this exchange. I have absolutely no recollection how long we stood there. Eventually we, that is to say "our side," were brought to another, smaller room.

Stacks of clothing—not striped this time—just gray sacks and wooden shoes, were flung into the corner. Wooden shoes is, maybe, too fancy a description. Actually, all they consisted of were wooden soles with some straps made out of some very rough material nailed to them. Someone handed each of us one piece of underwear. I drew a longish man's under-shirt while Lotte looked funny in a pair of man's long-johns complete with a fly and a button-up rear, except that all the buttons were missing. We all must have looked adorable.

We were then told to get into the gray sacks, to tie those shoes onto our feet and we were now ready for whatever awaited us. We marched out of the building and into the thin early morning light. We marched not back to the camp but toward the train platform. An empty train was standing there, and we were ordered to get aboard.

I don't think we were ever happier climbing into anything. It was the usual cattle wagon train complete with the *Scheisskübel*. And, once aboard, as always, we waited.

Two things about that day remain vivid in my memory: It was a beautiful morning with a slowly lifting fog and the sun breaking through, and the agonizingly long wait for the train to pull out of Auschwitz. It seemed to take forever, and we were naturally scared to death that we would be called back to the camp, that the whole thing was only a make-believe. But in the end, the train began to move, oh so slowly at first that it was almost unbearable. It chugged through the now familiar entrance arch and picked up speed and finally passed the last of the buildings and the fence. The many tracks converged and became one, and we were indeed on our way, and it didn't matter at all that we had no idea where we were going. What mattered was just getting away from this hellhole and much less that we might wind up in another one.

Again we stood with our eyes glued to the cracks in the walls of the boxcars through which we caught glimpses of green fields, dark forests and woods, towns and villages, all flying by. All I could think of was, "Please God, let me never ever come this way again!" We were all very quiet, afraid, nervous, and thinking about the group we had left behind. Someone called out the names of the cities we passed, reading them on the signs of the railroad stations and we realized that we were going west, toward Germany. We rode for about a day, stopping occasionally, perhaps at a traffic signal or to take on water and coal for the locomotive. Finally the train halted at a small station. "REICHENBACH" (now Dzierzoniów) read the name on the station platform. The doors of our cattle cars were opened, and their contents, about 175 of us, piled out into a warm early evening. It was not quite dark yet and there seemed to be a golden mist spread over everything. Perhaps it only looked golden to us because we were away from hell.

Orders were barked at us, and by now we knew what they meant without actually understanding a word of them. We lined up and stood as straight as we could. A couple of uniforms and, to our surprise, a few men in civilian clothes walked slowly by inspecting us. Another order, and we lined up five abreast and started to march. The station was close to the town of Reichenbach itself, which looked to us like heaven with enticing and well-kept houses on both sides of the street on which we marched. The gardens in front of the houses were full of apple and pear trees and it was then and there that I promised myself to eat as many apples as I could if I ever got out of this nightmare.

We left the residential area of the town and entered what obviously was the industrial section with large and rather rundown factories, a bombed-out station with some burned-out boxcars next to it, some sizable warehouses, and then an enormous and not too ugly looking factory. A plaque next to the entrance proclaimed, *Gebrüder Kohn—Weberei* (Brothers Kohn—Weavers). That was our destination and our next place of work.

Even though, as the plaque read, brothers Kohn had been manufacturers of woven materials, the looms were now gone, and in their place were machines that manufactured electronic gear. We were briefly welcomed by a tall handsome man in a white lab coat. This short but pleasant interlude was immediately followed by a uniform barking an order, and we were on our way to a small camp with just two barracks and one latrine. That first night, though, we slept outside the camp in a barn filled with straw. It was the most wonderful night's sleep we had had in a long time. The contrast between the Auschwitz barrack, and this barn was enormous. The barn was warm, we had room to stretch out, and the straw smelled great.

Next morning we were yelled awake by a short woman in a long SS cape with a voice that could cut through steel. She had huge breasts and buttocks, and she was our new commandant. She told us that she used to be a *Puffmutter* (a brothel mother—in other words a "madam") and at first we found it hard to believe, but as time wore on, and we got to know her better, we more and more believed her and accepted her version of her past.

That morning we started to work in the factory we had seen the night before. First we were given the usual battery of tests and then groups of us were assembled and assigned to different parts of the building. The remaining group was given additional tests and then subdivided into still more groups that were assigned to different machines. By this time only a handful of us, myself included, remained and stood out. I was not happy about it because we all had learned that the less one was noticeable, the better. More tests were given us and then just two of us, Paula and I, remained standing and waiting.

A young man came over and beckoned us to follow him into a room full of machines, oxygen tanks, optical equipment, microscopes, and other precision instruments. He began by motioning to the optical equipment and, without saying a word, proceeded to show us how it worked. Paula and I grew perplexed, and she finally asked him in German why he couldn't just explain the mechanics instead of pointing and grimacing. He looked at us as if we were little green Martians. *"Sie sprechen Deutsch?* [You speak German?]" he squeaked.

He was flabbergasted to discover that we were not *Untermenschen* (subhumans—that is, Poles or Russians) and it took him some time to recover from that shock. Günther Behrends turned out to be one of the nicest men I had ever met and it took us little time to discover that his attitude toward Hitler and Nazism was not radically different from ours.

Chapter 9

Bombs and Beets

Our first day in that vast factory was bewildering. We had to learn a lot in a hurry, orders were yelled and screamed at us from every direction and by all kinds of people, and, most acutely, it was hard to find the toilet. In due time, as it had heretofore, the toilet played an important role in our life in Reichenbach. But that was later.

Paula and I were assigned, together with some Russian and French prisoners of war, to the room with the optical equipment. It was a vast hall the ceiling of which was the roof itself, which, along with one wall, consisted of glass panes all painted black to prevent any light escaping and being seen by enemy planes at night. The huge room contained two sections. Optical equipment was on one side while on the other stood long tables supporting what looked like long sewing machines along with some intricate looking machinery. A sort of a glass cage that turned out to be an office, stood in the middle and in front of that an enormous table. Toward one end of this vast hall, the height had been divided horizontally and a second-story laboratory installed. Paula was assigned to the optics department. I was taken to a huge machine in the other part of the hall where I joined some Russian POWs.

There was a German civilian *Aufseherin* (guard) who was to be addressed as *Fräulein Scholtz*. Miss Scholtz was a blond, out of a bottle, and she wore very short and very low-cut dresses and high heels and turned out to be the dumbest blond I had ever met. The list of things incomprehensible to her was endless. Most puzzling to her were the facts that I was Jewish and for that reason was put in a concentration camp, that I was Dutch but could speak German, that I had blue eyes while being a Jew and, even more perplexing, that I knew what to do with those big and intimidating machines without anybody's supervision or instruction, a fact that was, of course, very useful. Realizing that she herself had not the faintest idea what this big machinery was designed for, I could, right under her nose, help Günther Behrends build a short-wave radio on which we were able to receive BBC broadcasts. But that came later.

The head of our department was a smallish man who looked so much like an owl that we instantly named him *die Eule,* (the owl). I still remember his real name, Abel. Then there was Erich, not my old enemy but a brand new Erich who was thin, small, and cross-eyed, with legs forming an almost perfect hoop, who must have had at one time or another far too many drinks, which colored his oversized nose a bright purple. He was certainly not a handsome man. Erich was an outspoken Communist, who didn't care at all whether anyone knew it or heard him talk about it.

But ugly, hoop-legged, cross-eyed or not, Erich became the dream of *Fräulein Scholtz* who did everything imaginable to attract his attention. She sprayed herself with quantities of a perfume that must have been designed to keep anybody, even flies, at a safe distance. Her dresses be-

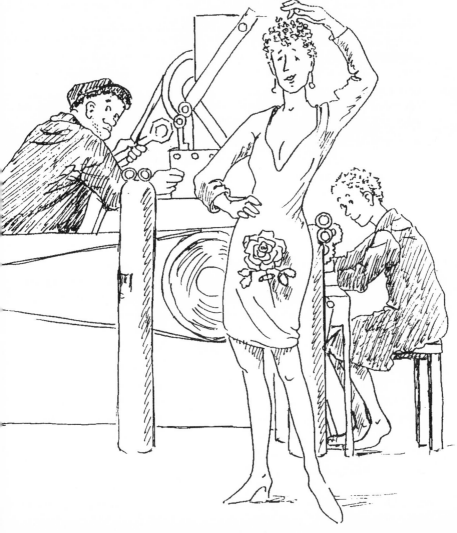

"Du Erich, guck mal!"

came lower and lower at the top and higher and higher at the bottom. Then, one day, she thought she had found the perfect formula, the perfect bait. She pinned a large red rose right in front, at a very suggestive spot on her skirt, wriggled her hips and called out, *Du Erich, guck mal!* [Hi Erich, give a look!] He did, and that was the last time he paid any attention to her as far as I could see. I couldn't help feeling sorry for her.

The man right under the Owl was Herr Kindler, a very nice and quiet human being who taught us—me, the Russians, and the French—how to use the machines and the related equipment.

Our group occupied one of the two barracks in the small camp, about ten minutes' walking distance from the factory. There was also one latrine and a nonelectric wire fence around the compound. On one side of the camp was an empty field, on the other was a farm. Close to the wire fence were rows upon rows of carrots. As soon as we could and as far as our arms could reach, we would pull the carrots out and eat them. But the supply of carrots seemed never to run out. It finally dawned on us that the kindly farmer kept refilling the empty carrot holes with fresh ones just as soon and as fast as we had "organized" (our word for stealing) them. We never saw him, and we could never thank him but let me do it here and now. He may have saved some of us from near starvation.

The barrack was locked at night. That in itself was not so bad because by now we didn't mind the constant air raids anymore, and we were aware that we could be hit by a bomb as easily in a barrack as in a so-called bomb shelter. But what did matter was the fact that we could not get to the latrine. We got one *Scheisskübel* in the barrack, but it was no bigger than a common pail, I mean, again an ordinary household cleaning pail, and it was filled in no time at all and overflowing in all directions. Every morning we had a rather nasty lake of no mean proportion in our "entrance hall." For whatever reason, our *Puffmutter,* Madam, or, if you will, commandant, displayed a profound dislike for Judy, one of our girls, and made her clean up by herself that mess every morning in time for our departure for work. No one was allowed to help Judy.

Nobody wanted Judy to be saddled with this stinking occupation and therefore a solution had to be devised. We decided to forgo the *Scheisskübel.* The windows seemed to offer the alternative. They could be opened, and one could even lean out a bit, at least till stopped by the exterior iron bars in front of them. We learned to "go" by way of the windows, iron bars and all. Our *Lagerälteste* Bertel, and another woman had a small room with one window, also outfitted with iron bars, all to themselves. Bertel, as the head of our group, gave us a lecture to the effect that we were not allowed to use windows as makeshift latrines, but she failed to tell us what we should do instead. So, the window parade continued. I did wonder what Bertel and her roommate did in case of "need" but it didn't worry me too much.

Then one day, while we were marching to the factory, a German guard happened to be marching next to our row and he said, in a typical Berliner accent to no one in particular, *"Na. . . Eure Lagerälteste hat auch noch nen schönen dicken Arsch, wenn die so aus dem Fenster macht* . . . [Well . . . your camp-elder still has a nice fat ass, when she's hanging it out the window to do her business]." Thus that riddle was solved, and the windows kept doubling up their functions.

Our Puffmutter.

The roll call one morning had a new twist: Our *Puffmutter,* from her long experience with ladies of ill repute during which she acquired her vocabulary, looked on us as just another batch of ill-reputed ladies and her first command in the morning was, *"Raus aus der Furzkapsel!* (roughly, Get out of the fart capsule!)" After we made our beds, or *Furzkapsel,* military-style, came the second command: *"Raus aus dem Puff!* (roughly, Get out of the whorehouse!)" The third command, again in her loud, hoarse, deep voice, was *"Bauche rein!* [Stomachs in!]" Being from the Sudetenland, she spoke with a heavy Slavic accent. That order, as well as the next one, *"Brusten raus!* [Chests out!]" was really unnecessary because by now we had neither any bellies nor breasts to speak of. We tried our best nonetheless. She walked up and down the row with all of her ample features sticking out. She sported the German female guard's uniform of long *Hosenrock* (culottes), mannish-cut coat, and a long, long cape. Topping the outfit was a uniform cap, and she wore the black high boots of the Nazi uniform. She was as wide as she was tall. The coat buttons could not contain her abundant bosom, and the cape kept constantly sliding off her shoulders and dipping in the mud, of which there was a lot in Reichenbach. She really was a fantastic sight, and I, for one, tried to stay as far away from the first row and from Floortje as possible because I had enough trouble keeping a straight face without hearing Floortje's wisecracks. By and by we realized that the Madam didn't mind being stared and grinned at and tended to disregard any remarks she might have overheard.

Once she was certain that none of her charges had somehow escaped during the night through the locked doors and slipped by the watchdogs unnoticed, she would utter the next command, *"Los essen,* [Now eat]." We lined up to get into the kitchen where Roosje was dishing out the food, which was a true delicacy compared to what we ate in Auschwitz. Here we had some kind of a pasty cereal in the morning, a piece of bread for lunch in the factory, and some soupy stuff in the evening. Three meals a day—unheard of. After the breakfast at about 6:30, it was off to work. We worked twelve hours a day, from seven in the morning to seven in the evening.

There were some five main departments in that huge factory with many subdepartments in them. Our group was spread throughout the place, and we worked alongside Russians, French, Poles, and other nationalities. Most of them were prisoners of war. If there were any Jews among them, we did not know it.

The first few weeks were confusing. The constant commands and air raids added to the confusion but within a short time we got used to both and ceased to pay attention to them. Each of us was handed a small square piece of blue cardboard upon entering the factory. It was our one and only "toilet pass," good for one visit. These blue squares of cardboard were guarded with our lives. At first we tried to "hold out" for as long as possible and then we used them only as a last resort. But later we found some blue cardboard boxes in which light bulbs were packed for delivery and from that day onward the blue-pass business became a highly profitable one.

My machine was a fairly complicated piece of equipment that was supposed to manufacture parts for very small radio transmitting tubes, even smaller than the P. 500 that we made in Vught. The assembled tubes were about half an inch high and quarter of an inch in diameter and contained some thirty parts, and they usually didn't work. By and by it became my job to find out why these tubes refused to function. I was taken off "my" machine, was invested with the title *Einrichter* (something like an engineer) and was off to my new and exciting profession of which I knew as much as a cow knows about laying eggs. But, of course, this I kept to myself. I put on a very intelligent face and looked at those darn machines and the brand new and useless tubes. Günther Behrends, realizing that I was fairly in a thick fog, taught me as much as possible in the short time period. Thanks to his instructions, I learned to fix the machinery, so it could produce more or less functioning tubes. Then came the real blow: I turned out to be so efficient and reliable, thanks to Günther's guidance, that I was put on the night shift and in the same position that Günther held in daytime. That meant being separated from my friends and walking back and forth by myself while being watched over by a male guard, a female guard named Gretel but affectionately called "the cow," a "nurse," who was a Jewish prisoner also named Wiesje, and, of course, our friendly German shepherd, Freia.

I had to be at work an hour before the end of the day shift in order for Günther to show me all the machines that had broken down during the day and had to be fixed. And believe me, there were at times more broken-down machines than working ones. I had to work an hour longer so that I could return the courtesy to Günther. Of course, as soon as I got one of those monstrosities fixed and got one of the Russian POWs on it, the darn thing broke down again. I did not have to be a genius to realize that between the broken machines and the tubes that failed to function, we had a run of sabotage on our hands. Lovely, as far as I was concerned. But to keep both the sabotage and the machines going simultaneously, while saving my own and everybody else's necks, was a juggling act. I felt quite like a tightrope walker. Although they understood and even spoke German, the Russian girls refused to use it. So, I had to learn Russian to the great amusement and joy of my "teachers."

Actually, the night shift was not too bad. The factory was quieter. I ate with the prisoners of war whose food was a bit more appetizing, and my guardian angels fell asleep as soon as the drone of the machines started. The one thing that was scary during the night shift were the air raids. Since we were so close to the Russian front in Reichenbach, our nightly visitors were the Soviet bombers. All of us, myself included, my German guards, and the others, were more afraid of them than those of the Western powers. The Soviet planes would fly very low, humming like giant bumblebees, hover seemingly right overhead, and empty their bellies of bomb after bomb, rarely missing their targets.

In Reichenbach, at first we would follow orders and run out of the factory and head for the "shelter" as soon as the air raid siren wailed. With those interruptions becoming more and more frequent, less and less work was done and that suited us just fine. We had quite a distance to run to our air raid shelter, if you can call it that. Trenches had been dug between the graves of an old cemetery a little way outside the town. I remember feeling kind of funny jumping into those trenches and hoping the bombers were not too interested in a bunch of dearly departed. In as much as the cemetery's location was rather remote, we often reached it just as the "all clear" sounded. Soon the running to and from it became very monotonous. It also was very cold among those graves and growing colder with the eastern winter approaching. By now, staying alive didn't seem very important anymore. Freezing rain and snow became the order of the day and then, just as in Vught, we were surprised to find a big heap of old coats awaiting us in the barrack. This time I found a brown, rather nice and long ladies' coat. Even in our "nice" coats, we looked like ragamuffins with our scrawny necks and almost bald heads sticking out of the garments. By that time our heads were not shaven anymore but were sprouting some hair again. I am sure that our bare and thin legs and feet added little to our femininity, but then, as long as we were warmer, who cared? Paula became the owner of a green kind of leathery jacket.

Well, winter had arrived with a vengeance. The snow was not the most bothersome but the freezing rain and the ice certainly were. Then one night, while we were working in the factory, the air raid siren went off again. The Russian planes sounded somehow louder. There were definitely more planes than usual and the sound was ominous. My female guard, Wiesje, and I thought it prudent to get out of the building. The male guard didn't share our feelings, told us that it was pure *Weiber Feigheit* (female cowardice) and stayed with Freia, the dog, inside and probably went back to sleep.

Looking back at it now, he had had the right idea. But we—Wiesje, Gretel "the cow," and I—got out of the building. The rest of the night shift left the building through the rear entrance over the fields and proceeded toward the graveyard. I was working too close to the front entrance to make it all the way back through the enormous building, and so we got out the front door and literally landed on our buttocks. The street was one huge ice field, and we slid on our rear ends right into the middle of the street. Wiesje and I were the first to be back—more or less—on our feet. We did our best to get Gretel, the heavy "cow," back on hers but since she wore the high German leather boots and was about four times as heavy as we were, it was nearly impossible. When we finally had Gretel on her feet, the two of us, Wiesje and I, would fall down again. Gretel tried to get us up but by doing so she lost her footing and down she went too.

Bombs started to fall by now, and fire broke out all around us. The noise of the explosions and fire was deafening, and we could feel the intense heat. After see-sawing a few more times, we decided to call it quits. There was nowhere to get to anymore anyway, and the middle of an icy street was as good a shelter as anything else in the immediate neighborhood.

Wiesje had with her a large bag made out of some rags and inside it were all her worldly belongings. One of them was a tiny piece of bread. She divided it into three microscopic crumbs and the three of us, sitting there in the middle of the ice-covered street with bombs detonating and all sorts of debris flying around us, "enjoyed" our treat. All of a sudden, all of it struck me so funny that I started to laugh and soon tears were streaming down my face. The other two first looked at me as if I had lost my mind, then, after a few moments, joined in. The three of us, sitting there in the middle of the falling bombs, noise, burning houses, and screaming people, laughing our heads off, must have been quite a sight. Not that I think that anybody was able to see us. The air was filled with smoke, new fires erupted constantly, and the heat was rapidly getting worse.

After what seemed an eternity, the all clear sounded and we made our way back into the factory. The heat had melted the ice and the eerie glow of the fires had turned the night into a nightmarish day. By some miracle, nothing had happened to the factory. We just stood around doing nothing because there was no electricity and therefore no lights or power to turn the machines on. Finally the night was over and the day shift came in. They came with gruesome tales of the damage the bombardment had inflicted on that part of the town and that not much remained standing anymore. As a matter of fact, they had not expected to find a shred of the factory. When I finally left with my entourage, I saw that what the day shift had told us was actually a gross understatement.

With the usual German efficiency, electricity was promptly restored, and our machines could again start to spew out parts for the various tubes and other radio components. The only damage left from this attack was that the black-painted glass roof of the factory now had many holes, caused by flying bits of shells, exploding bombs, bricks, and other debris. So, with the roof no longer lightproof, the moment the siren sounded, lights had to be turned off, and we were, of course, unable to work, a fact the Germans disliked immensely.

To rectify this defect, some Russian POWs, all males, were brought in to fix the glass roof. Huge scaffolding was erected, enough, I'd say, to service the Eiffel Tower, and the roof-fixing got merrily under way. The men were hard at work up there, but progress seemed kind of slow. Nevertheless, the Russians seemed to have a good time whistling and singing Russian songs and not understanding, of course, any German-language command given them. It was all a great performance. The roof was finally fixed, and now it was decided to place bags filled with fiberglass between the rafters but, please, don't ask me why. I doubt, in fact, that anyone really knew the reasoning behind that decision. Maybe they had some fiberglass left over from a previous job, or just wanted to keep the Russians busy a while longer. They certainly didn't seem to mind it in the least. They kept on climbing up there, whistling and singing merrily, paying absolutely no attention to the yelling and shouting of their German guards.

There were, of course, also some Russian girls, POW's, among our group of workers and there was a small closet standing inconspicuously in a corner that did a brisk and steady business as a lovenest.

At this time I was back on the day shift for a short period working together with Paula on a special project, a huge sending tube, about a yard high. It was a combination of a pentode and an octode. We worked with molybdenum which has a very high melting point and we were supposed to melt iron onto it which has a much lower melting point. We were rather at a loss as to how to bring about such a miracle and found out later that we were not the only ones. The German workers didn't know either. Finally, after a lot of trial-and-error, we came upon the "brilliant" solution of putting a kind of mantel or casing around the molybdenum parts and melting the wire to it. That worked and was hailed as a major feat. But during the trial-and-error interlude, we hit upon another great idea: the molybdenum bars made for perfect safety pins, and the prisoners—Jewish or not—had a million uses for them. So pretty soon we had a steady business going. A simple safety pin was good for a little piece of bread, a blue toilet pass, or maybe even a piece of paper.

The Russians, meanwhile, continued working high up on the scaffolds, above our heads, putting the fiberglass-filled bags down. Then came an order to clean the place which meant, of course, that *hoher Besuch,* (high-ranking VIPs), were expected. A few days later some high-ranking uniforms indeed appeared. But, as we found out later, this visit was only a preview. These officers came to inspect whether everything was ship-shape, fit for even *höheren Besuch,* (higher-ranking big shots), and they came in and walked slowly around, running their fingers over the machines to check for dust. I made the mistake of looking up toward the Russians on the scaffolds and under the roof still busily putting those bags down. But two of them held one of the bags upright and started to open it. I had the feeling that things would soon liven up, and I found it hard to suppress my glee in anticipation. I was right. The two of them up there started to sprinkle fiberglass down on the uniforms. Some of the nasty stuff found its way down the backs of the officers. Quite obviously they tried to ignore it at first and, as befitted typical German officers, kept their backs straight, chins up, and all the rest of it.

But the fiberglass proved too much for these tough cookies. Soon they started to twitch, and their shoulders started to move in a very unofficer-like gestures. Suddenly, they gave up the inspection and disappeared. It sure would have been interesting to learn how they ever got rid of those irritating fiberglass particles, but I suspect it may remain a secret forever. The *hoher Besuch* arrived a few days later, and this time even the Russians behaved themselves.

A very large and fat woman in the uniform of an *Obersturmbannführer,* her ample bosom highly decorated with ribbons and medals, arrived to inspect the factory. She looked mean, somewhat like a bulldog afflicted with gallstones. She was accompanied by a large entourage of clearly high-ranking officers. Her title and name was Fräulein Obersturmbannführerin Dr. Hildegarde Klabund. Quite a mouthful, I know. She had small, immensely sharp and intelligent eyes and I doubt there was anything that escaped her notice. She didn't say a word. Her all-male entourage kept a respectful distance and watched her every move. She only had to flick her fingers or make a motion, and somebody was immediately at her side to explain or take orders. She must have been a really big, very big shot. In any case, she was awe-inspiring, and we were plenty scared.

After inspecting the machinery, she looked at us. As she passed slowly in front of us, we got the feeling that she not only looked at each of us but through each of us and that once she had seen you, she would never forget you. It was the first of her many visits.

Our *Lagerälteste* and Dr. Kohn had been working very hard in the meantime on getting "our" other women who had been left behind in Auschwitz, to join us. And, finally, through Dr. Kohn's powerful connections, I guess, and out of the sheer need for more workers, the effort succeeded. Thus, in the middle of one night, we heard voices and shuffling footsteps, and we realized that our friends had arrived. We were overjoyed, even if only briefly. There developed almost immediately a rift between the two transports, and though I can't put my finger on it, I suspect that tensions were unavoidable in the somewhat clannish and defensive behavior of all of us. The rift continued for a long time. The new arrivals were housed in the heretofore vacant second barrack.

After a few months in Reichenbach, we were issued new numbers to replace the ones tattooed on our arms that were now no longer valid. Up till now we had been under the jurisdiction of the Auschwitz concentration camp and as *Aussenkommando* we were ordered to work outside the camp. But everybody who was punished—like Saantje, who could no longer hide the growing fruit of her love affair with the "beautiful" Erich—or anyone suspected of sabotage, was sent back to Auschwitz, or more precisely to Birkenau and its gas chambers. But now with the new numbers, while we were still *Aussenkommando,* we belonged to Gross Rosen, another concentration camp in that part of the Third Reich, and were under its jurisdiction. Our new numbers were written on a small, round piece of cardboard, which we wore on a string around our scrawny necks. More significantly, we were ordered to remove our yellow stars and in their place to sew on a red triangle that changed our status from Jew to political prisoner. I don't know why this was necessary. Perhaps the Germans wanted to show that the Jewish "problem" had been solved and that the Third Reich was finally *judenrein.*

Close to our small camp was a larger one that was a German military base. I believe it was a Luftwaffe installation. The two camps shared a common kitchen but not the food. Theirs was fit to eat. But they needed workers in that kitchen, and a lucky few of us were commandeered to become kitchen helpers in addition to our regular work. I was one of the "lucky" ones along with my friends, Elli and Rita. We were marched in a small column from our camp past a few guards and their dogs toward the camp kitchen, where we came face to face with the largest red beets I had ever seen. They were cooked in immense kettles, and then we had to peel and slice them. The kettles were put on the floor where seven or eight of us would sit around them peeling and slicing the cooked beets while another group was at the other end of the kitchen peeling and slicing cooked potatoes.

Our physical condition was pitiful. I doubt that any one of us weighed more than 80 pounds or so. Our diet of watery soup, one square inch piece of very dark bread, and once in a while a treat of a so-called *süsse Suppe* (some sweet concoction called soup) had reduced our figures to sticks. Our breasts had completely disappeared and now we had found a reason to be reasonably happy about the "loss" of our busts. Carefully, so that we wouldn't be caught, we'd put a half of a beet where in better times we'd sport a breast. It was not too easy to keep those things in place, and the beet juice stained our one and only garment. But we were hungry, and we knew that there were two barracks full of hungry friends, so we took the chance. It all went quite well for a few days. The guards were not interested in us so quite a few beets were smuggled in this unusual manner to be divided so that everybody got a thin slice of this delicacy.

One day, coming back from the kitchen we encountered a new guard. It was totally unexpected, and before we had a chance to get rid of our newly acquired bosoms, we were face to face with him. Thank goodness Floortje was in our group, and I am sure she wouldn't have been afraid of the devil himself had he suddenly appeared before her. She stepped up to the new guard—she towered over him—and stroked him under the chin while we paraded through the gate, beet bosom and all. It almost went without a hitch. But Elli had put some of the boiled potatoes into her pants, which she had gotten when we were presented with our one piece of underwear in Auschwitz. In her haste to get past the guard, she must have taken too large a step and began to lose her potatoes. It was really very sad to be losing those valuable potatoes, but it sure was a funny sight to see them dropping to the ground. And, once again, Floortje saved the day. Calmly, she picked them up, gathered them into her skirt and marched past the guard, red bosom and all.

Unfortunately, we did not get away with it this time. We were not summoned back to the kitchen. It was the end of a promising smuggling enterprise.

Chapter 10

Christmas 1944

In Reichenbach we had a modest *Krankenstube* (infirmary) with about ten beds that tended always to be filled as long as there were no *hoher Besuch* on the horizon. Even a rumor of *hoher Besuch* approaching was enough to empty the beds because any illness was deemed sufficient cause to be sent to the gas chambers. With us, since Auschwitz, was a very fine Polish doctor named Halina. A tall, enormously intelligent, and efficient woman, she had studied at the Sorbonne in Paris. We did not know why she—a Gentile and a physician—was in a concentration camp even though we were aware that she was not an exception. But we, and especially I, were lucky to have her with us.

A half of a tube of Bayer aspirin and a kitchen knife were all she had at her disposal to heal the sick. There were no drugs, medications, thermometer, or bandages. Nothing. But she knew how to brew teas out of half a dozen leaves and roots, pound paper into bandages and perform miracles with a kitchen knife. I don't think she ever "lost" a single patient. Dr. Halina was truly a healer.

Sometime at the beginning of the winter I got quite sick, and so did Inge. I was in the *Krankenstube* for about a week. I know I was delirious for a couple of days because, as I was told later, I bewailed the loss of my sex appeal. I don't know why this should have been important to me one way or another, since I never thought I possessed that attribute to start with. We had, by now, been reduced to a haggard and very tired bunch. Being ever more weakened meant that it took ever greater effort for us to perform the same work. The clothes we wore, the solitary piece of underwear, no stockings, some old rags that had been issued to us instead of the gray sacks, and the coats, were woefully inadequate for the bitter Eastern European climate and the unheated barracks. Consequently our efficiency must have been equally inadequate.

We felt we needed something to cheer us up. So we put together a sort of a cabaret. We did a few skits. Somebody did a great parody of Hitler. A few had some funny routines a la Stan Laurel and Oliver Hardy. We invited the *Aufseherinnen* to the shindig and, to our surprise, they enjoyed it, even—maybe most of all—the parody of the Führer. By now it was Christmas, 1944.

Our "protectors" did a noble thing and gave us a day off. We made all kinds of plans for, after all, this the first free day we had in a long time! But, as the saying goes, "The best laid plans of mice and men. . ." We slept. I mean, we slept through the whole free Christmas Day. Which means we slept right through two nights and a day. Don't ask me how this was possible. Somebody must have awakened at one point or another and realized that it was daylight. Maybe it was just too much to think, much easier to go back to sleep. Whatever the reason, we all slept for thirty-six hours.

The next day, of course, it was back to work at the factory and the old routine. I had become quite friendly with some of the Russian POW's, especially with a nice looking tall girl named Sonia who fell in love, deeply in love. Not with one of her Russian coprisoners or even a male of another nationality. No, she fell in love with Paula's green jacket. It was something she absolutely had to have. The Russian POW's were still rather human looking. Their bodies were still bodies and not just dry sticks hanging loosely together like ours. Sonia made herself a bra out of wire. Something like two little baskets connected with another piece of wire. I seriously doubt this contraption was comfortable but Sonia, unlike us, was ready to endure a lot for her "beauty." Anyway, she felt that Paula's green jacket would be the crowning glory and thus the bargaining started. Sonia had a black jacket that was much warmer, longer and roomier than Paula's green one. But it was older, not as elegant—at least in Sonia's eyes—and it was black.

I know that Paula didn't care one way or another, but she did enjoy the bargaining. In the end she did wind up with Sonia's black jacket plus a toothbrush and half a soft roll with sugar on it. When we were liberated and brought to Sweden, we looked through our clothes, ripping them apart before they were burned to see if any money had been sewn in them. Paula found several pound notes sewn into the lining. In any event, Sonia, meanwhile, had her *veston verte* (French for green jacket) and was deliriously happy.

While most of us worked all this time at one machine or another, Inge, simultaneously, had quite a different career which began early during our stay in Reichenbach. The German head of her department was one Herr Kinder, a mean, nasty, little man. Why he disliked her from the beginning was a mystery, but dislike her he most emphatically did. So he put Inge into the most degrading job he could think of, namely cleaning the prisoners' toilet. It must have been a horrible job. Most of us were sick by now, and we were only allowed to go to the toilet once a day, at least before we found the blue cartons and fabricated our own toilet passes. We had diarrhea and who knows what else. Most of us, in order to avoid physical contact with somebody else's nastiness, put our feet on the rim of the bowl, squatted and let our "business" drop in or out of the toilet, on the rim or on the floor. It sure was an awful job, and she had to do that all day long, twelve hours a day.

All Inge had was cold water and a rag. No soap, no brush or any other cleaning stuff. Her travail lasted for seven or eight months until we left Reichenbach. The only good aspect of this whole dreadful business was that we had a reliable person at our news gathering spot, who could relay the news messages from one department to another. Usually the news came from our department where we had the radio.

Every so often during those months, we had visits from Fraulein Dr. Klabund, and they hardly ever deviated from their pattern, and we thus got used to them and were not frightened anymore by them. But—and for me this was a very big but—she fell in love with me. Why? I certainly had not the slightest idea. Dirty and scrawny, I must have looked awful. Nevertheless, she picked me to heap her love upon. She called me into the glass-cage office and told me that she would make an *Ehren Arier* (honorary Aryan) out of me, that after the war she would be my mentor and lover and would get me bras and girdles, and I would have, in other words, heaven on earth.

I was scared to death, believe me! When she found out that I could draw, she brought me colored pencils and paper. It sounds funny now, but then it was anything but.

New Year's Eve came and so did snow, icy winds, and bitter cold. We repeated and expanded our "cabaret" and the next day we had *süsse Suppe*. Well, on the basis of our experience in previous camps, this signaled some change. We were sure we would be bidding goodbye to Reichenbach but had no idea where we would end up this time. The grapevine had somehow broken down again. The next day was the coldest we had experienced so far. While we were on the roll call, we heard the news that we were being transferred to the "*Sportschule,*" a work detail of Gross Rosen, the concentration camp, and that was bad news. The *Sportschule* used to be just that, a school for all kinds of sports. It had been transformed early on into a concentration camp that acquired a sinister reputation. In a valley close to the Riesengebirge (Giant Mountains), a range that had separated Germany from Czechoslovakia until Hitler's takeover in 1938, the camp was in the shadow of the Eulengebirge (Owl Mountains), and about one and a half hour walking distance from Reichenbach.

It was a bitter cold morning. The wind was constant and blew easily through our thin clothing. Our legs became sticks of ice in no time. We had lost our tin bowls in Auschwitz and had been eating out of some kind of crockery soup dishes while in Reichenbach. Now we were handed those, and our march to the *Sportschule* began. The road was wide and covered with a sheet of ice. We were sporting our wooden-soled sandals, and I am sure it would have been easier to walk on ice skates.

The guards tried at first to keep us in rows of five in neat and straight columns, but since they found themselves unable to walk the icy streets without slipping, sliding, and falling down just as we did, they soon gave up, and everybody walked or slid the best they could. It didn't take long before all the crockery plates were broken which made the task of proceeding a bit easier. But once we were out of the built-up section of town and entered the wide valley in front of the Eulengebirge without protection against the icy wind, the walk turned into sheer horror. Some of us crawled on all fours while a few held onto each other, but this did not prevent us from sliding and falling. We were more down than up, and the one and a half hour walk turned into an exhausting five-hour-long nightmare.

It was dark when we finally reached the *Sportschule*. We were in something resembling Auschwitz but on a much smaller scale and without the crematoria and the stench. Two-story high dirty gray build-ings were inside the compound which was surrounded by electric wire and closely spaced watchtowers with their blinding, white, and revolving searchlights that cast an eerie light over this scene. A female voice was bellowing at us. We stood, it seemed like forever, on roll call in the bitter cold and were completely frozen and numb by the time we were finally allowed to get inside the ice-cold barracks where we, the girls in my par-ticular group, drew the second floor.

There, in a room in which every window was broken, we found some fifty bunks, stacked two high. There were straw "mattresses" on them, and some of us got thin blankets. It was so cold that as many as possible got into as few bunks as was possible and we used the mattresses from the empty bunks as covers on top of the few blankets that could not pos-sibly have kept us warm.

The following day the sun shone brightly, but it still was bitterly cold. We were called to roll call and now got a chance to see better our new quarters. The screaming female voice of the previous night belonged to a horrible witchy-looking woman. Everything about her was black: the uniform, the hair, eyes, and the by no means small mustache she was sporting under her nose. She had some accent, Czech or Polish, for which she compensated by being nastier and noisier than any commandant we had had so far.

The dozen or so barrack buildings that had really been used at some time as dormitories for the school of sports, were spaced pretty far from each other and the wind was howling like mad among them and around the corners. Some buildings were larger than others. There were also two latrines and an officers' building. Somewhere in the background was the kitchen and, smack in the middle of the camp, the *Effektenkammer* that contained clothing, blankets, and other useful things denied us. It was a small building with an A-roof, a low and wide chimney, and it was, of course, locked.

Close to the electric fence were the latrines, makeshift affairs, just a long trench dug into earth and a round, very slippery bar to "sit" on. You had to hold onto those things with all your might so that you didn't tumble into the mess underneath.

In this, our new "home," we were together with Hungarian, Polish, and Czech prisoners All of them worked in Reichenbach. The Hungarian girls were young enough to be still children, and they worked in the railroad depot cleaning out boxcars. They had found some newspapers and wrapped them around their emaciated bodies against the bitter cold. Our hearts went out to them. Then, one day, the black witch-commandant found out about the newspaper undergarments and almost killed one of those children, beating her with a heavy stick until the girl fell down. The girl had fainted but the big brute assumed she was dead, and left her alone on the ground. The poor little thing came to after some time, and I prayed that she'd come out of her ordeal somehow alright. But it wasn't until many years later that I learned that my prayer had been answered.

Our downstairs neighbors were Polish girls, and there was no love lost between us. I don't know why we disliked each other, especially in light of the fact that we didn't even know each other. I suspect that contributing to the hostile climate were the surroundings, the atmosphere, the overwhelming hatred, and the lack of any normal human emotions. The girls downstairs worked in a factory close to ours, but I don't recall what was being manufactured there.

Life, if one could call it that, in the *Sportschule* was simply awful. In retrospect, this period seems to have been worse than Auschwitz. Perhaps it was due to the bitter cold winter at a time when we were already so weakened, or maybe everything really started to look so hopeless and there was no end in sight, not one way or another.

Roll call was, as usual, very early, and in that cold seemed endless. Then came an almost two-hour-long march to the factory, which suddenly seemed cozy, warm, and friendly, and was like coming home. Also, by now, air raids were increasing in frequency, and they became so much a part of our existence that nobody really bothered to run for cover anymore, not even when we heard the Russian planes overhead. Simultaneously, a factory in or near Berlin had been bombed out of existence, and we were supposed to take over its production and pick up the slack. Accordingly, large crates of machine parts arrived one day, and a few of us were commandeered to assemble whatever it was supposed to be— without any directions, guidance, or even hint. We had no idea what this equipment was, what it looked like or its purpose. In short, we hadn't the foggiest and neither did our guardian angels. Nonetheless, we opened the crates and looked at the assorted pieces and, lo and behold, in one of the crates we found a blueprint, which didn't do us any good because several crates containing many more parts were missing.

But to show our good intentions, we proceeded. After all, the German motto was, "Nothing is impossible." Soon enough we came face to face with the first big problem: no tools that fitted the particular screws and bolts that were supposed to hold this thing together. Herr Kindler got some metal and undertook to teach me how to make tools. It's not an easy trade to learn, but I got good at it, and what's more, I enjoyed it.

A few guards accompanied the crates from Berlin to Reichenbach, and, for some reason, they stayed around. One guard in particular was constantly watching and seemed to be counting the parts as we lifted them out of the crates. It seemed funny at the time, and we wondered whether he believed that we could walk out of here with a 5-foot-long piece of steel dragging behind us or carrying a 25-pound wheel under our arms. He was interested not only in this particular piece of equipment but also in everything that we did in each part of the operation and especially in what was happening in the white room, where the large sending tubes were being assembled, as well as the operation of the optics department. He was present at all times and made us more than a bit nervous.

Then one day, while standing next to Paula, he said something to her too quietly for me or anybody else around to hear. The whole incident was strange because the only way German guards seemed able to communicate was to scream at us. After a while Paula came over to me but did not mention the incident, and something told me not to ask her. It was about three days later, that she wanted to talk to me in the latrine. And there, sitting next to each other and trying to keep our balance on the frozen, slippery, messy bar, she told me that the guard was an English spy or, at least that's what he gave her to understand. That, of course, could have been a trap. He could have been a German undercover agent, an agent provocateur. The next day he was gone, never to be seen again. I personally heaved a sigh of relief and only then realized how jittery this man had made me. Still, I often wondered who he was, if he was really a British spy and whether he survived.

Time seemed to stand still while we were at the *Sportschule,* and I remember the feeling of being completely suspended and cut off from life itself. With the camp located far out of town, we—on our way to and from work—rarely saw anyone not connected directly or indirectly with the camp. Incidentally, it was invariably dark when we marched to and from the factory. The stillness and emptiness heightened the feeling of isolation and it was in the factory that we had more or less a feeling of reality. Our work there, however, started to become disorganized. Parts that were needed did not arrive. Machines broke down and couldn't be repaired and we did not have the parts or tools we needed to make those repairs. There were no bottles of gas or oxygen for the welding apparatus. All this made us uneasy, for, after all, what good were we to the Third Reich if we could not produce? Whether it was our fault or not.

The machine parts were not the only freight that never reached Reichenbach. Food became scarce. It never was much to start with but now it became almost nonexistent. Once a day we received a ladle ¾ full of some soupy slop that was thinner on some days than on others. We never dared to inquire what made the stuff thicker but frankly at this point we couldn't have cared less.

Our barrack would get one large soup kettle, more or less full, which we, the Dutch group, had to share with our downstairs neighbors, the Polish girls, with whom we shared a mutual dislike. It was a rather intricate procedure. We had an empty kettle and since we, the Dutch group, usually had the pleasure of schlepping the full one from the kitchen to the barrack, we also divided its contents. I know that even though we didn't much like our co-occupants, we were scrupulously honest in measuring their portions and ours. Then one day the downstairs people went to the kitchen to get the food. I don't know whether they were commandeered or whether they "volunteered," but they went and got it. They asked for our empty kettle to divide the slop.

There were forty of us upstairs and sixty-five girls downstairs. Five shared one ladle of "soup." This meant that we received eight and the others thirteen ladles. Before they started to divide the stuff, there was a conference among them. In Polish, of course. They seemed to enjoy something they had hatched out, and with grins on their faces they went to work. The ladles were counted carefully, and they obviously had a

A small victory over the miserable slop.

splendid time doing so, a rare sight indeed in the *Sportschule.* When they had emptied eight ladles into the second kettle, Rosje Klein stepped forward, motioned to somebody to help her, got hold of the kettle that was being filled, said "Thank you, these are our eight portions," and with a straight face and the help of some of us, carried the soup can up to the second floor. So far we really didn't know what had transpired. We only sensed, judging by their bewildered look, that something unforeseen had happened to our downstairs neighbors. Once upstairs, Rosje burst into laughter. Having been raised in Poland before moving to Holland, she was fluent in Polish. The Polish girls wanted first to ladle out thirteen large portions for themselves, leaving eight small ones for us. But since they didn't know Rosje understood them they had miscalculated, and we were "enjoying" eight large portions of the miserable slop, leaving thirteen little ones for them. It was a small victory for us.

Our friend Lea worked in the department of Herr Kinder. Unlike our department's *Eule,* this man was a sadist and a Nazi through and through. Lea had been made "foreman" on a rather large machine, which stamped out small mica chips the size of a nickel, which held together the different parts of a radio tube. She tried to make the work somewhat more efficient and easier for her coworkers and in the course of doing this, she accidentally jammed the machine. When Kinder found out, he put Lea on report.

She was "tried" and found guilty of sabotage. The penalty for this offense was "death by shooting or hanging." Usually the prisoner was allowed to choose. We were frantic. All of us expected to be killed any minute of every day. We saw death around us constantly. But this was different. This was happening to Lea, one of our "family."

At this point Dr. Kohn intervened. How she did it I don't know. None of us knew. But somehow she got through to Berlin, very high up, I'm sure, and the sentence was changed from sabotage to *Übereifer,* being overanxious to work. Instead of the death penalty she was to get fifty "*Stockschläge,*" beatings with a cane. Our bitch of a commandant had the pleasure of personally administering the penalty. I am sure she enjoyed it no end. Lea did not utter a single sound during the proceedings. Afterward she was more dead than alive, but she was still with us. She never showed me her back. I wanted to try putting compresses on it. There was enough snow, and we could have somehow "commandeered" some old rags or paper, but she wouldn't allow it.

There was one other nastiness. When Lea was taken to the *Schreibstube* (the commandant's office), for her punishment, the guards removed her jacket and did not return it to her. To be without a coat or jacket in this bitter cold was a certain death sentence. Again we were panicky, but we put our heads together and came up with a plan. It was a dilly. We decided to go and "lift" a coat out of the *Effektenkammer,* the small building standing right there in the middle of the camp. The idea was great but looking back at it now, also completely crazy. And perhaps because it was so asinine, it had a chance.

The revolving searchlights bathed the small, one-story building, standing quite isolated in the middle of the camp, in bright light every few seconds. Getting to the building without being seen by the watchtower guards would have been a feat of no mean proportion. Nonetheless we were determined to get to it and lift out of it a coat for Lea.

Lore Blank, the thinnest of all of us, volunteered to get down the chimney into the building, grab a coat and climb back out. The question then was how to get her onto the roof and then, if miraculously she made it in and out of the chimney, how to get her off the roof. The only way we figured this could be done was to "build" a human pyramid for Lore to climb up and pull herself onto the roof. Once there she'd have to crawl to the chimney and somehow get inside it and down into the building. Next, one of us would also have to reach the roof and the chimney and pull Lore out of it and then both would crawl back to the edge and over the roof and down the "pyramid" and, finally, we'd have to make a safe return to our barrack.

The seven "strongest and tallest" among us were selected to build the pyramid, and were ready the next dark and bitter cold night. I was one of the "chosen," but I will honestly admit that I didn't feel too brave or confident that night. We raced, one by one, during the split second of darkness that the searchlight permitted us, toward the *Effektenkammer*. We huddled together once we made it to the narrow side of the building which did not get quite as much light as the other sides. Next came the circus act of forming the pyramid at which we were not very adept. But with a lot of trial and error, a lot of pulling at each other and pushing each other up onto somebody's shoulders, we made it. Lore climbed up and finally stood on the shoulders of someone on top and with the searchlight's beam turning away made it onto the roof and to the chimney. I was one of the "bottom" girls and therefore did not see any of this.

As Lore told us later, she let go of the chimney's rim and to her surprise landed softly on a table, piled high with clothes, that stood right under the chimney's opening. The same searchlight we were so careful to avoid proved to be a boon to her inside the dark building as it provided enough light to see a chair, which she put on the table. She grabbed what felt like a coat and with a bit of stretching was able to get hold of the chimney's edge, pull herself up and again waiting for the opportune moment when the light was away, get out of the chimney, reach our "pyramid," and make it to the ground. We all raced back to our barrack, and only when we were safe inside did we remember the cause of it all, the coat. Lore was wearing it, a heavy black kind of a pea-jacket. We were a happy bunch. We had pulled it off. Lea had a coat.

The next day we went as usual to the factory. It was a cold, bright day. I was still busy producing tools and had just finished a small wrench. I had drilled a hole in the middle of its handle so it could be hung on a nail and just then I heard the planes, obviously Russian. By then, though, we were so used to their noises that we just didn't pay much attention to them. I do know that no alarm had been sounded. Suddenly there it was: Bombs started to drop on the factory; the noise became deafening; smoke was all around us, and people screamed. I stood motionless. I don't know whether I could have moved but, thank goodness, I looked up, and there the whole big window that also served as part of the wall was falling as if in slow motion toward me. I'll never know what made me raise my hand, which held the little wrench I had just made, as if to hold up that huge window-wall. But the glass shattered on the edge of the wrench. Pieces of glass, large and small, rained around me showering splinters in every direction. When the cascade finally settled I was still standing in the same spot I had stood when the window came crashing down, and there was not a scratch on me.

I stepped as carefully as I could over the pile of glass and through the now glassless window frame and out into the factory yard. People were huddled or running all over the place. Looking westward we saw fires and smoke coming from several factories, and the bombs were still falling. Finally the planes turned east, and the all-clear sounded. The air raid wardens probably were anxious to correct their error of not having sounded the alarm in the first place. We were called together, counted, and by some miracle not one of the prisoners was even hurt.

One girl told us that she was standing in the middle of the factory working on one of the bigger machines close to the pedestal with a bust of the Führer on it, and the first thing that was hit by the bombs, she added, was that bust, and Erich who was near the machine had said, "*Na Gott sei dank, der Hund ist 'runter.* [Thank God, that dog is down]."

Anyway, the guards were told that there was only one way open to get us out of Reichenbach. One bridge was still intact, and I guess they were ordered to get us out and over that bridge as quickly as possible. They made us run down the street, past burning buildings and factories out of which people were streaming and heading with us for the bridge. Many of the girls and women from the other factories lost their lives in this raid that came barely a few months before the end of the war.

Once over the bridge, we marched toward the camp with very mixed feelings: elated that the factories were out of production and very apprehensive of what would happen to us next. On the one hand, unless we worked, we were of no use to Hitler. On the other, officially at least, we were now prisoners of war and not the damned Jews anymore. Back in the camp, we were allowed to get into our barracks. We were sitting around trying to guess what lay ahead, preparing ourselves for the worst, hoping that once again we would somehow get out of this turn of events alive.

As it got dark, we were called out for roll call. It was again an icy cold evening. The stars were glittering with a bluish sheen. I remember how very big the stars looked. We seemed to stand for hours. Finally the commandant appeared with her underlings, and she told us that the next day we, all females, would leave the *Sportschule.* We were also given the good news that we were allowed to take our blankets along. That was an additional break even though the blankets were as thin as plain cotton sheets, and there were not enough of them to go around. At least they would not present a weight problem. The uncertainty of what was ahead was more than offset by the prospect of leaving this hell-hole.

Chapter 11

Across and Inside Mountains

Early next morning we were whistled awake and out of the barracks to stand on roll call. Somebody came and dealt out some bread and then disappeared. Each of us got a nice chunk of it to our delight, and there we stood. Everyone who had secured a blanket had it rolled up under her arm. No one showed up for quite some time, and we began to wonder what was going to happen next. We had expected to see our witch of a commandant but she never appeared. At last the next in command arrived and ordered us to form a *Kommando,* which was a column of rows of five abreast. This SS officer was not too bad a guy.

We started to march out of the camp and toward the Eulengebirge, a section of the Riesengebirge. I was very lucky to have wound up, by sheer chance, in the first row. We were not the only ones to leave the camp. Germans, all or most of them as far as we could determine, were leaving with us but there was no trace of our hairy witch of a commandant, and we certainly didn't miss her. If anything, we were still afraid that somehow she would suddenly reappear. But she didn't, and to this day her fate is a mystery. There were guards all around us, and our long column snaked slowly through the snowy valley toward the mountain. The snow was high, the wind was blowing full force, and the mountain seemed to recede farther and farther. We were told that we would climb over those mountains and come down on the Czechoslovakian side. We did eventually arrive at the foot of the Eulengebirge, and looked up in disbelief and even shock at the steep slopes and the winding, narrow road and wondered how on earth would we ever be able to climb it. We were bone tired, weary, and had no muscles left to help us climb. By this time the column had lengthened with long intervals between rows. The guards tried to keep us closer together but with very little success.

Soon we did begin the tortuous climb up that winding, narrow road and within thirty minutes or so we were all out of breath, ready to give up and about to fall flat on our faces One or two did collapse and were shot dead on the spot. There was one additional factor contributing to the difficult progress up that road. We were following a herd of cows which were leaving behind tangible proofs right there at our mostly bare feet, green, slippery and plentiful. At first we tried to sidestep the dung but it was of no use. And here we discovered one more proof that one can get used to anything, even fresh cow manure liberally sprinkled on an icy, snowy, slippery, sloping road. We could not see far ahead of the road due to its serpentine course, and thus we came suddenly face to face, or rather face to rear of an immense herd of cows. In the distance that we could see, there were just cows and their herders, a rough and tough group of men speaking a foreign language.

The road was barely wide enough for five of us to walk abreast and sometimes not even that wide so there was no way for us to get past the cows, which were clearly ignorant of the Third Reich, Hitler, or the need to obey one's guards. They just ambled along, and then once in a while they stood still or even lay down, and their herders were obviously in no particular hurry either. At first our guards tried to talk to them and then yell at them and then bargain with them, but to no avail. We were behind the cows, and that's where we remained for the next two days. It was our luck that the bovine herd went slowly and ploddingly up the mountain, taking frequent rests and forcing us to do the same. Furthermore, the snow was being trampled and packed down and generously coated with manure rendering the road rather slippery but our feet, at least, were not sinking up to our bare ankles or even deeper in the snow.

Halfway up the mountain, I started to feel sick. My head began to throb, and I knew I was running a fever. I was very scared because anyone who couldn't keep up with the column was, as we had seen already, shot on the spot. I felt progressively worse and more scared. I got so terribly ill that I really no longer cared one way or another. But my friends did. They pulled and coaxed me along but it was very tough going despite the cows and the slow pace.

The mountains were high and climbing them—even when one was well fed and felt rested and strong—was no picnic. It was dark already when we somehow finally reached Neurode, a tiny mountain village. We were put up that night in several different quarters. Again I was lucky because "my" group, which included Dr. Halina, drew a horse stable that was warm and full of horse manure. One of the girls told the physician that I was sick, and Halina came right over to me, felt my pulse, and confirmed my suspicion that I had a high fever. She gave me half an aspirin, part of her most valuable treasure, and proceeded to pack me into and cover me with the abundant horse manure. She then told me to lie still so that the stuff wouldn't roll off me and promised that I'd be as good as new the next morning. I remember how absolutely awful I felt with every part of my scrawny body aching and how I shivered. Slowly, though, I started to feel warmer and finally fell asleep. When I woke up the next morning I felt perfectly fine. My fever was gone as were my aches and pains. Dr. Halina had kept her word and me alive. Now, whenever I don't feel well, I long for her and a stable full of horse manure.

Soon, on a beautiful day with a dazzling blue sky against the white snow, we were on our way again, and so were the cows. The landscape all around us was magnificent, and once we reached the crest of the mountain range, we could see Germany to one side and Czechoslovakia on the other. It was a sight I'll never forget. It gave me some hope. There was so much beauty that simply could not be destroyed, not even by Hitler. We followed the serpentine road. At almost every curve there were small wooden triangular *Heiligenhäuschen,* or holy shrines, with a beautifully carved figure of either Christ or Mary sheltered under its A roof topped by a high pile of snow. It was strange that the snow didn't slide off the steep sides of the roofs.

At around noon the cows and their "drovers" settled down for a rest, and so did we. We ate a tiny piece of bread. We did not know how long our bread was to last. And now we ran into a new, if minor, problem. So far when mother nature called, we could at least retreat behind a tree, having dutifully gotten permission from the guard and our guard dog Freia. But here and now, above the tree line with nothing but mountain ranges, snow, and cows with their herders in sight, there was no privacy, no place to hide, and we did the best we could, simply closing our eyes to the indignities to which we were more than accustomed.

Dusk was falling as we entered Braunau, but it was still light enough to see that it was a beautiful little town. We walked the length of its main street where people in drab and colorless clothes, women with babushkas framing their faces, watched us silently. Once again we halted at the outskirts at a large farm where we were once more divided into several groups and assigned one of the many empty outbuildings. That night our group slept in a cow shed.

The third day in the mountains was as beautiful and clear as the previous two. Only when we resumed our march did we realize that our cows had left us, and in light of the start of our descent this was no great loss. But we did miss them a bit especially the trampled-down snow. The road, hewn out of the rock, became narrower and the curves more tortuous. Soon we passed caves, and as we descended into the valley we observed that the caves were occupied and served as housing. Here and there one could sneak a look into the gloomy interiors. To me those caves looked cozy and warm, and I was jealous of those cave dwellers. Now, in retrospect, I'm sure that those caves were anything but ideal living quarters for humans.

We reached our goal, Adelbach, after dark. We were again divided, and some of our girls slept that night in a castle. Also quartered there was a group of Russian men, prisoners of war, and I think one could write a book about the experiences of those girls, experiences that they themselves admitted, were not all unpleasant.

Our group was assigned to a big and welcoming barn. We had to climb to the hay loft through a square opening that was no more than three or four feet across. The hay was dry, thick, warm and smelled wonderful. The only nasty thing was that square hole in the middle of the floor and I'm fairly sure we all slept rather uneasily, afraid to fall through it. The owners of the barn were a lovely couple. They spoke German with a heavy Czech accent, they offered us some bread and something hot to drink, and showed us an outdoor spigot so we could wash as well as an outhouse, the greatest luxury on this four-day journey. I often think of these nice people and thank them with all my heart for showing us that there was still some humanity left in the world. We said good-bye to our hosts with some sadness, and once again marched off in a long column beneath a sky that was growing gray and getting darker by the minute toward an unknown destination. There was an unmistakable smell of snow in the air. Around noon, a sharp, icy wind sprang up, and soon it started to snow. It fell so thick and heavy that at times it was impossible to see past the first few rows of people, and when we arrived late in the afternoon in the town of Trautenau, or Trutnov, we were icy cold, wet through, and completely exhausted.

Our quarters were the four floors of an old, unused chocolate factory that had been converted into a prisoner of war camp. The large halls were crowded with bunkbeds and were painted a poisonous green, so vivid that whenever I see a large wall painted green I am immediately brought back to Trautenau. We were assigned bunks on the fourth floor, given some hot soup with some real vegetables floating around in it, and afterward we shed our sopping wet clothes for the first time in a long while. We went to sleep under blankets that had been piled up on the bunks.

Next morning we found a shower room with some warm water trickling from the shower heads. It was a wonderful luxury to feel the warm water on our bodies and we all felt clean, which I'm sure we were not, a sensation we hadn't felt for months. Security was so relaxed that I don't even remember a single guard during our entire four-day-long stay in the chocolate factory. I did some mending for myself, since I still possessed a needle, and for anybody who needed it.

It snowed steadily outside, and I know we all wished we could stay there. We didn't want to think about the future and felt that the present, such as it was at that moment and place, was better than what we had had in a long time.

A part of the building was occupied by some Polish and Czech girls. They seemed to feel very much at home, which led me to believe that they had been there for some time already. A circular staircase, rather narrow for such a big factory that must have employed a large number of people at one time, led from our top floor to the floors below and to the basement. Inge and I went exploring and found some Polish girls who had set up a shoemaker shop. We were amazed by what these girls could produce out of nothing.

I suspect that despite all their planning, the Germans didn't exactly know what to do with us, which suited us just fine. We had a four-day vacation, and in my memory it was exactly that, a vacation. Nothing, however, lasts for ever, and after those four days we were told to get ready. We were moving out and since we had nothing to pack, this was an easy order to follow. We, as usual, felt apprehensive and even sad to leave the place.

It was still snowing, thick flakes tumbling down from a dark sky. As we left the chocolate factory, we got the first glimpse of our new commandant, a smallish man in a green SS uniform. We couldn't have known it then, but we were lucky because he turned out to be one of the nicest commandants; in time, we came to call him Papa. With him were some new guards, also in SS green.

We marched in rows of five abreast to the railroad station, but it was snowing so heavily now that we were almost on top of it before we saw it. A tremendously long train was waiting which was not unusual by itself. What was unusual was the sight of roofless freight cars, sand or coal cars actually. A thick blanket of snow covered the bottom of the cars and the whole thing did not look to us inviting in the least.

Someone counted rows and stopped at the twentieth. The first group of one hundred was ready to "board." Each of us got a chunk of bread and some salty canned meat. "My" group was in the first car, right behind the coal tender. In addition to the Philips group, there were also the girls who had resided in the chocolate factory when we got there. The snow kept falling so thickly that we could hardly see the next car or even the locomotive.

With the help of several shouted commands, we clambered into the open "cattle" cars, and our feet sank in several inches of snow. It didn't take long for the snow to become a deep, dirty messy slush. In no time at all we all looked like snowmen, and we realized that soon we would be soaked and should it turn any colder, we would all freeze to death. Finally the train started to roll out of the Trautenau station, and we headed in a northwesterly direction. It kept snowing but fortunately it didn't get colder. And being in the first car that close to the engine was certainly a bonanza for our group of 100. We could feel some of the warmth of the fire, but with it we also were getting some of the sparks. We were standing, tightly squeezed together, and after a while we were getting bone weary and tired. Then one of the girls, Stella, had a brainstorm. Why, she asked, didn't we split up 50/50. One half could lie down and sleep while the others would squeeze themselves around the rim of the car and keep time by counting two hours, say, and then we'd reverse the order. The idea was brilliant, the thought of bedding down in the nasty slush on the floor less than inviting. But it was still better than passing out from exhaustion. It worked, and we took turns sleeping and standing day and night, and the other wagons followed our lead. We were wet and cold and very hungry because not knowing how long our rations had to last, we hardly dared eat any.

The train ride was not a smooth one. The tracks and bridges of the once efficient German railroads were in shambles. The sporadic bombardments made sure they stayed that way, and our train had to wait for crews to fix whole stretches of tracks as best they could, which usually wasn't very good. To our left and right we saw burning cities. We stopped more times than we proceeded, and our train ride lasted several days and nights. Outside Leipzig our train stopped again. Three Greek girls who had escaped from some concentration camp train joined us. They couldn't get anybody to help or hide them, so there was nothing else for them to do than to join some prisoners again.

Every so often clusters of planes appeared and emptied their bellies, usually at a little distance from us but then one day at one point while we were standing on an unusable track, bombs started to fall a bit too close for comfort, and one made contact with our locomotive. Not close enough to blow it and all of us up but enough to put it and the tender out of commission. Miraculously nothing happened to any of us. But we were now stranded somewhere in the middle of nowhere, and it was still snowing and, what was worse, it was getting colder. My legs felt frozen. I had no feeling whatever in them, and to this day I have on each leg a large spot of frostbite that has never healed, but it could have been worse.

We were keeping up our routine of standing, counting, and sleeping. After a night and half a day, some workers finally showed up, uncoupled the cars from what was left of the tender, and we were pulled away. After another long wait, our cars were hooked to another locomotive and our trip resumed.

We choo-chooed around Berlin, passing countless small stations. We stopped at one of them, Belzig, where we got some water to drink. Being hungry is bad enough but being thirsty is worse. The few snowflakes we had been able to catch were not enough to quench our thirst, which was worsened by the salty canned meat.

It did finally stop snowing, and soon afterward we were on our way again. The signs on the more or less damaged stations we were passing through started to bear familiar names The last time we passed them was on our way to Auschwitz. We remembered Hannover well and how angry we were that the city looked so beautiful, untouched by the war, its surroundings green and well-kept. We didn't have to be angry this time. Hannover was now in shambles, and even the snow could not hide the fact that little of the city, as far as we could see, was left except for bomb craters, burned down houses, and scorched fields. When we pulled into what had once been the grand train station of Hannover, we were greeted by hanging girders—blackened and twisted steel that had once supported a majestic glass dome. There was an eerie quiet and desolation. No people could be seen. All around were burning houses, flames shooting skyward, and heavy smoke hanging over everything. Somewhere past the station, the locomotive took on some water, and on we went.

That night we arrived at Bergen-Belsen, which we knew to be a very large concentration camp, and we assumed that it was to be our newest "home." But we were also aware that it was by now more than overflowing with prisoners, and the prospect of becoming a part of this overcrowding did not lift our spirits. Several officers came down from the camp and spoke to our commandant. After that, some kind of a soup was brought down and, as in Auschwitz, each of us was allowed to take a few sips. The soup was warm, and it tasted delicious to our starved taste buds.

Bergen-Belsen was not destined to be our new quarters. Early next morning big vats of a hot drink resembling coffee were brought to our train but Papa, our commandant, did not let us drink it because he had found out that typhoid was rampant in Bergen-Belsen. The weather, meanwhile, was steadily improving and getting warmer. On the last day of our open-car excursion, the sky was blue. We maintained our schedule of sleeping and standing which was adopted by those in other cars, and thanks to it we made it finally to Minden in no worse shape than we did.

It was afternoon when our train pulled into Minden, and we were ordered out of the cars. Our legs were stiff as boards, and we could hardly move. Still, out of habit, we lined up five deep and stood more or less at attention. Our commandant, Papa, walked past us and to our utter surprise, told us that we should relax. He added that we were not at the end of the line and that we had to walk the rest of the way to Porta Westfalica, a camp under the wing of Bergen-Belsen. So we started to walk and pretty soon two things became quite obvious. The first, that it was very difficult to walk on a pair of legs that absolutely refused to do any such thing, and the second, that the "walk" turned into a climb at the first turn in the road, and the climb got steeper by the minute. It was sheer agony to climb even a yard up that mountain, and none of us thought that we'd ever make it up to our new abode. But Papa set a very slow pace and waited for anybody who had to rest, encouraged, and even helped some of us once he realized that the going was too tough. My legs just didn't seem to respond; they started to hurt, my calves felt as if they were on fire while I had no feeling left whatsoever in the other parts of my legs.

Slowly and painfully we conquered that winding road. It was getting dark when we passed by a large opening in the face of the mountain, inside of which we saw some wooden construction that reached into the darkness of the *Stollen*, (the mine shaft). And from between the wooden beams, and out of what appeared to be holes bored into the sides of the mine shaft, faces peered at us, faces of young girls, children really. They looked at us, quietly, wary, and even hateful. Anything new must have been threatening to them, as it was to all of us, and so we were to them who had been there probably for some time.

We continued our climb and soon found ourselves on a high plateau. The road had widened and now followed the crest of the mountain, curving through woods where it was covered with a deep layer of dry leaves. The wonderful scent of decaying leaves and the swooshing sound of many feet trampling the thick layer of those leaves made me forget for a moment where I was walking and why I was there. Actual walking was easier here even though my legs continued to hurt. Either the pain had lessened, or I had gotten used to it.

It was dark already when we finally reached the camp, and we were greeted by the smell of newly sawed wood. We lined up in front of a long low structure, which we came to know as the officers' staff building. We were quickly assigned to barracks, and what's more, were allowed to enter them. They were, to our intense joy, new, clean, and quite large. We could choose our bunks, and Inge and I took a lower one while Elli and Lea settled on the one above us. Two to a bunk, as usual, but now that was fine because we could keep each other warm during these still cold nights in early March.

The Porta Westfalica camp had been built to accommodate troops, which had never arrived there. The bunks were as new as the barracks and so was the toilet, which had, to our immense astonishment, partitions between the individual "potties." It all seemed exceedingly unreal. Of course it was very late by the time we had more or less settled down and a bright moonlight streaming through the windows illuminated our new "home."

The lice-infested "Stollen Kinder."

That first night, however, was not as peaceful as we had hoped it would be. The bunks were not built very sturdily, probably done in haste and with a minimum of material. We were exhausted and fell asleep as soon as we lay down in our bunks, but were awakened by a crash—a bunk had collapsed. Soon another followed, and another, and suddenly Inge and I found Elli and Lea along with several pieces of wood as our bunk companions. It was a miracle that we all got away with just a few minor bruises. The four of us scrambled out of the bunk, started to collect the usable pieces of wood from the upper bunk, inserted them into the lower to reinforce it and make it a bit more sleep-worthy, and the four of us—from then on—slept together in the lower bunk. The only difficulty arose in the morning. We had to put the wood back hurriedly into the upper bunk, make that one up in a military fashion, with the neatly squared corners of the light blankets, do the same with the lower one, and be ready in time for the roll call which was early as usual. And, as usual, we stood five-deep outside our barracks and got our first daylight view of the camp.

The barracks were camouflage painted. Beautiful tall trees, mostly oaks, surrounded the area and some even stood tall inside the camp. We got a small portion of bread and were told that we would get our meal in the mine shaft. We then marched off to our workplace, taking the same road back that we traversed to get to the camp the night before. Upon arriving at the gaping doorway leading into the bowels of the mountain, we were ordered in. This, then, was our current destination, our new place of work. The wooden construction we had seen the previous day supported some bunks, now empty as were the shelves dug into the earth of the mountain. The *Stollenkinder,* (mine-shaft children) as we came to call them, were already at work. A long corridor had been cut into the mountain, and stairs led down to several levels, all outfitted like a factory.

Somebody told us that we were now working for the *Hammer-Werke,* which had been a large company in Germany even before the war. We were divided into groups, assigned to a foreman and a work area. As we walked toward the latter, I glanced at the machinery. It looked very familiar, and I was quite sure that I had seen it all before. I had. It was the old Philips machinery, some even had a few of our names scratched into them. Many of the bearers of those names were no longer with us. I was put to work on a long monster of a machine that was supposed to manufacture radio tubes from A to Z without any help from mere mortals. It was not a Philips relic, and only God knows where it came from. This long thing was designed to put molybdenum rods into gliders, wind wire around them to fashion grids, push one grid into another, then add a cathode and an anode and, voila, the tube was finished. The trouble was that the machine didn't do anything of the kind. Whatever I did to fix it, or whatever the foreman, who, incidentally, knew less than I did, tried to fix, the machine stubbornly refused any and all help. If, by sheer luck, one part of the thing worked, it broke down somewhere else. We stayed in Porta Westfalica for four weeks and never once did this long contraption give birth to one single radio tube. Maybe it felt like doing some sabotage of its own. Some of the girls worked the vacuum pumps, some even on the very same machines they had worked on two years earlier in Vught.

Our stay in this camp was quite different from anything we had experienced heretofore. The commandant was a very kind man, and the guards took their cues from him. He was concerned about our health to a point where he begged us to "please" sit down on the toilets so that the rims wouldn't get dirty and also not to eat the garbage that was thrown out of the guards' kitchen. But his pleas fell on some very deaf ears. The toilets didn't stay clean very long since some of the ladies felt that things could be accomplished better in a squatting position above the rim, and we were so starved and food was so scarce that we all got into the garbage to find potato or vegetable peels which we prepared and "cooked" in the washroom. It was not a brilliant idea because many of us got very sick from this fare.

Shortly after we had settled in, the *Stollenkinder* had to pack up and move in with us. They had mattresses on their wooden shelves in the shaft. Those mattresses had to be moved to the camp. Moving day was beautiful and clear. Early spring was in the air. The trees and fields showed their first delicate greens. I remember a patch of violets among the trees.

Not only mattresses but also all kinds of things had to be carried from the mountain to the camp. I was entrusted with a big box, filled with odds and ends, which was hard to handle and which got heavier with each step. A few rows in front of me and to the left was Rosje Klein carrying a mattress and trying to balance it on her head. She stumbled over a rock or stump, and she and the mattress fell to the ground. Suddenly a guard appeared and started to beat down on Rosje's head with a heavy stick. The beating was so vicious that I doubted Rosje would ever get up again. Someone restrained this madman, and we kind of carried and pulled Rosje back to camp. Later, it took months in a Swedish hospital for her to recuperate. But this was the only incident during our stay in the Porta Westfalica camp that was reminiscent of our former experiences.

One day, on our way to work, we came face to face with a large herd of deer. I think they were as startled as we were but showed no fear at all. After a good look at us, and I'm sure we were quite a sight, the herd just ambled away. Somehow I had the feeling that a few of them were shaking their heads.

When the *Stollenkinder* joined us, they brought along lice. Body lice at that. So far we had been lucky and had made our acquaintance only with fleas. That was bad enough, but lice? That was a horse of a different color, and that was bad!

First of all, lice are carriers of diseases such as typhus and trench fever. Next, they are the itchiest things around and so small that it is quite impossible to catch them. They also multiply astronomically, and we were scared stiff that we would be infected with typhus, which we indeed were. Papa tried to do something about the lice. From somewhere, he ordered large kettles, which were set on stones and filled with water. Fire was built under them and it took for ever for the water to come to a boil. When it finally did, we were ordered to put our clothes into the boiling water. In as much as we had no other clothes than the ones on our backs, the entire operation was a big gamble. After all, the well-worn material could easily have disintegrated in that boiling broth. I wonder what we would have done in that event. In any case, while our clothes were being boiled—perhaps washed for the first time in who knows how long—and afterward hung on some branches to dry, we were running around in our birthday suits trying to keep warm. This procedure—well-meant though it involved lots of work and a great big mess—lasted for three days, what with changing and heating water and drying the clothes outdoors.

It proved utterly useless. The lice survived and loved it.

Chapter 12

Beendorf and Gypsies

The entire month of March that we spent in Porta Westfalica was fortunately warm and pleasant. Inge's and my birthday is in March, and therefore we decided to "celebrate." So, we all saved the tiniest piece of bread from our daily ration, and when I say tiny, I am not kidding because our whole ration consisted of the chunky one-inch-square-size piece of very dark heavy stuff. On Inge's birthday, which falls three days before mine, we fashioned a "beautiful" cake out of those crumbs and some water and decorated it with leaves and violets. We all shared in this delicacy. It didn't taste any different, of course, from the junk it was made of in the first place, but it was nonetheless a birthday cake!

We spent our days that month deep inside the mountain working in the mine shaft and emerging only in the evening to return to our barracks to sleep. By now, we had no way of knowing what was happening during daytime but the nightly air raids became more frequent, and our sleep was increasingly interrupted by the wail of the sirens. We had to get up, dress, and go outdoors which certainly was no safer than the inside of the barracks. As the raids came closer and closer together, we decided to end the charade of undressing and went to bed fully clothed.

One night, a bomb scored a direct hit and exploded right in front of the mine shaft's entrance, thereby sealing it off completely. Luckily, it happened at night when everybody was already asleep in the barracks, and no one was inside the *Stollen*. With it knocked out of commission, we were out of work. The next two days we wandered around aimlessly with growing apprehension about our immediate future. Everyone kept asking herself, "What next?" Then came the order, "*Antreten* [form a column]."

After being counted, we marched away from the Porta Westfalica camp, again through the beautiful woods, past the now closed *Stollen* and down the mountain toward a waiting train. It was April 1, and it was rather warm, even hot, and we had, of course, closed cattle cars. But Papa was good to us. He posted guards inside the wagons and ordered the doors to be left open so we could get some fresh air. Only someone who has been transported in a closed cattle car knows what a truly good deed this was. As usual, our destination was a complete mystery.

So much of the once efficient and meticulously maintained German rail network had been bombed to pieces that it took forever to get from one place to another. We would arrive at a freight station to shuttle back and forth from one siding to the next and then wait for hours for usable locomotives, red lights to turn green, semaphores to go up or down, and tenders to be filled with coal or water to be consumed by the locomotive. We were hot, without food or water, and most of us had become sick with diarrhea or stomach cramps. All of us were terribly weakened.

On a warm and brilliant day we rumbled into a very large freight station, the name of which I don't remember, which seemed strewn with empty and obviously abandoned boxcars, damaged locomotives, and tenders. Whatever the reason, this was an excellent place for Papa to give us a little change and let us stretch our legs. Some of us went exploring inside this large place, and we found a boxcar filled with big barrels full to the rim with herring salad that provided a tempting sight and smell but which turned out to be badly spoiled. Even so, Papa had a hard time keeping us away from it. Without these efforts the salad could have easily put all of us out of our misery. And after that outing, we were not allowed out of the cars anymore.

After crisscrossing the land, mostly in an easterly direction, for about ten days, we arrived in Beendorf, which is in the middle of the salt-mining district of Germany. We marched away from the station and toward a tall tower. From afar it appeared as if the tower was in the midst of a rather disheveled-looking wooded area, which, upon a closer examination, turned out to be an enormous net, painted and covered with branches, a huge camouflage. Underneath it was a vast building now serving as a concentration camp. Prior to World War ll, it must have been a beautiful, exclusive, and expensive health spa, which, I'm sure, only the privileged could afford. With its exterior completely covered with the nets, there was now no way to see how the entire building looked. But the interior, even though ruined by having been transformed into a concentration camp, still showed signs of its former grandeur.

There was an immense, all white marble hall into which one entered through large ornate doorways at one side of a wide corridor. On three walls of the hall were very large and beautifully decorated windows, most of which were now missing their glass panes. That did not detract, however, from their beauty and elegance. There were some thirty large, octagonal, marble basins sunken in the floor. I am sure that at least ten people could easily have taken their "health" bath in each of them. In its heyday, this must have been a grandiose establishment.

Now the splendor looked rather ridiculous. All along the wall were wooden boxes with a round hole cut into the top, and a pail inside—our toilets! And we, in our rags, were sitting on the marble floor or in the marble basins. After a while, we were summoned to form a column in the hall, as always five in a row. At one end were some girls ladling out soup, which turned out to be surprisingly good tasting. After that we were brought into our "bedrooms." Some wooden structures had been added helter-skelter onto the original building. The rooms, if that's what you could call them, looked like huge packing crates stacked together without much planning. The bunks, four on top of each other, were wobbly and with our weak legs were hard to climb up and into.

There were quite a number of other prisoners already in the camp, women and girls from all over Europe. Most of our group stayed together in one of the large, high, boxlike structures. The rest of our group was mixed in with the earlier arrivals. It was a challenge to find your way in this place. Doorways had been cut here and there into walls without any "architectural" planning. At nights we were allowed to use the "toilets" in the large marble hall. The difficulty was in finding your way first to the hall and then, after being lucky enough to accomplish that, back to your particular packing crate and finally to your bunk

Inge and I decided to venture forth together the first night we were there. We slept in the second bunk up and coming down was luckily no problem. We held hands and crept between the rows of bunks toward what we thought was one of the doors leading to the hall. However, we ended up at a blind wall with no doorway anywhere. Then we tried to backtrack only to lose our bearing completely. We were not the only ones trying to find the toilets. In a short time everyone seemed to be wandering about, looking for the elusive exit. Most of us were, after all, suffering from diarrhea. Somehow, though, we did make it, but it was, all in all, a very active night.

The following day we were allowed to go to the latrines which were located somewhere behind the spa building. They were large affairs with an A-roof, no walls, just four corner posts supporting the A-roof. Lengthwise down the middle ran a deep ditch, on either side of which, running the entire length of the latrine, were two round poles, attached to the upright poles that supported the roof. The poles were tightly occupied by females all in great need of the facility. They held on to the horizontal poles to balance themselves on either side of the ditch.

As I was hanging on for dear life, with seven or eight others on one side, I heard a deep voice from the other side observing in Dutch, "Right now I shit smaller *balletjes* (marbles) than the diamonds I used to wear!" The voice sounded very familiar and, half turning on my precarious perch, I looked at the owner of that voice but couldn't recognize the face. Nevertheless I called out the name I thought belonged to that voice. "Marianne?" She looked at me and, of course, didn't recognize me either. There is a difference between, say, 125 pounds, hair, decent clothes and a washed face, and 70 pounds, chopped off hair, rags and a face crusted with dirt.

"I am Eva Hellendag," I said to her.

"*Eva?*" she cried out and almost lost her balance. We hadn't seen each other for over three years. She had lived next to my aunt in Amsterdam, and we had all been good friends. She had come to this camp with another group of prisoners and was housed with that group in one of the many packing-crate structures. But in this unbelievable labyrinth of structures, hallways, etc., it was hard to find one's way just to the places we had to go and much less manage to pay a visit. So I did not see her again. But this chance encounter with an old friend from another world gave me a tremendous lift.

Following the breakfast, the contents of which I have forgotten except that it was junk, we fell into our routine column of five abreast and headed for the mine shaft. A number of boxcars was standing there. They were filled with a pinkish colored, sandlike mass, which we learned was salt. It was waiting to be transported to wherever the Third Reich's war effort couldn't do without it.

The tower we saw from afar turned out to be the superstructure of the elevator shaft leading into the salt mine, a part of which was still in operation. The elevator consisted of two cages, one atop the other—primitive, open affairs with a floor, a low fence, and a gate and each capable of holding about thirty of us. The elevator descended 800 meters, about thirty stories, at a frightening speed, and I had the feeling that I had left a part of my body up there somewhere.

As we descended, we caught a glimpse of the mine. Here and there bright lights illuminated the most beautiful, colorful sight one could imagine. The huge walls of caves of the excavated portions of the mine were marbled in vivid blues, reds, and pinks with glittering white interspersed. It all glistened like precious stones. The deeper we descended, the hotter it got. The air was stifling, and fewer and fewer illuminated areas came into view. Finally, the cage came to a stop, and we all piled out. A guard with a lantern led us along a very narrow pathway hewn into the salt bedrock. At first we could walk upright but pretty soon we had to stoop and finally crawl on all fours. It was a long, hot, tiresome trek. Here and there we heard water gurgling near us while dim lights, mounted on wooden posts, picked out signs on the walls. One of them read "Magdeburg" with an arrow pointing forward.

We didn't seem to be getting anywhere, just creeping around like ants in the dark. Suddenly the tight and narrow tunnel ended on the floor of a huge cave, and we felt a cooler air. The cave was so high that the ceiling got lost in the darkness despite the light. In the cave were machinery, work-benches, and long rows of tables. Some men in civilian clothes stood together at one of the tables. One of them left his group, walked over to us, and, to our utter amazement, greeted us. It certainly was an unheard of occurrence, and only later on did we learn that it was Wernher von Braun. He joined Dr. Kohn and after a lengthy conversation with her called the rest of the civilians to join them.

In the meantime, the "old-timers" of this unusual working place had started to operate the machines and man the work benches. We were politely told to sit down at the tables, and then some of the men proceeded to explain to us what our task was to be: Work on the guidance system of the V-2. We had a vague concept of what the V-2 was—the flying bomb, the secret weapon that would surely help Hitler win the war and conquer the entire world. It was not a pleasant prospect to be working on this thing. Not, at least, until Dr. Kohn told us not to worry, that the systems would never work because the salt had undoubtedly damaged the metal components. Each of us got a tray filled with tiny parts, and someone showed us how to put them together. The light was poor, we had only a few tools at our disposal and, in general, the whole enterprise was quite chaotic. The work was intricate and nerve-wracking, made worse by the lack of light and tools essential in assembling the tiny parts. Once our shift was ended we faced the tortuous way back to the elevator. It was pitch dark when we finally emerged from the entrance to the shaft. But to smell and inhale the clean, clear, cool night air was exhilarating.

While down there, a group of women caught my attention. It was a small group, but it seemed very different. The women were big, strong, obviously well fed yet certainly not German or even Aryan looking. I couldn't understand their language, and what's more they were noisy and apparently unafraid of the German guards.

Our stay in Beendorf was cut short, again by a bomb. This time, however, it was during a daytime air raid, and we were 800 meters down below. The fabulous camouflage had failed, and it was a direct hit. The tower had disintegrated and with it the power supply. We didn't know or hear anything about the air raid, of course, but suddenly the noise of the machinery had stopped and everything was plunged into total darkness. It was frightening, and we all waited breathlessly, hoping that it was only a temporary power failure, which would soon be restored. But no such luck. It remained dark. Finally, guided by flashlights, we made our slow and difficult way back to the shaft, and there we suddenly realized that without electricity the elevators weren't going anywhere, and the only thing we could do was to climb up to the surface.

Hewn into the salt and rock all around the elevator shaft, clockwise, were stairs, about a foot wide and quite steep. On one side was the rough

The Gypsies.

wall and on the other side was nothing—the abyss of the now silent shaft. Somebody made us line up in the pitch dark and someone began to climb those stairs. Somebody spaced us so that we were not too close behind each other.

In front of me was one of the big and well-fed women I had noticed that first day. Somewhere along our climb, she told us that she belonged to a group of Gypsies. We climbed and climbed, constantly afraid that the salt steps would give way. We kept as close to the wall at our left as we could and for the first time we were grateful that there was no light whatsoever, and we couldn't see the gaping hole on our right. It took us about eight hours to reach the entrance platform and miraculously not one of us missed a step, and we all made it.

By the time the last of us appeared on the surface, it was way past midnight. An *Aufseherin* (woman guard), stood in the entrance of what remained of the tower building and said, "*Na ruht Euch mal ein bischen im Voraus aus* [Rest up a little in advance]." It was a cryptic command but one we gladly followed. At least the resting part of it. The "*im Voraus,* [in advance]," part held the promise of yet another change.

The promise was kept. We left Beendorf the next day. By now our number had swelled, and the column marching out of the camp appeared to be endless. An enormously long cattle train was waiting for us in the now demolished station. I don't remember how many of us were assigned to one boxcar, but we were able to sit down in it. This pleasant circumstance proved short-lived, however. There were far too many boxcars hooked up to the one old-fashioned and probably worn-out locomotive for it even to budge. Half of the cars were disconnected, and we had to double up. But to no avail. By the time the locomotive was able to pull the train, the number of boxcars had dwindled, and we were packed so tight—standing up of course—that none of us could move. It was dark by the time the train finally started moving, and we were completely exhausted, so much so that many of us just passed out and were held upright by the tightly packed bodies. Heretofore our group had managed to stay pretty much together. But now, with all the confusion of changing cars, being pulled out of one, and pushed into another a number of times, there was no way of knowing with whom we shared our moving sardine can.

Only in the morning, when it got lighter even in the boxcars, were we able to gain a vague impression of who our companions were, and there were not many of "our" group with me. Rosje Klein was somewhere in the middle, Paula, Lore, and Inge were close to me on one side of the car. And with us were six or so of the Gypsies. The train, we sensed, was moving rather slowly but we had no idea in what direction, and, at this point, we couldn't have cared less. We just wanted to get the whole thing over with.

For whatever reason, this was, I think, the lowest point emotionally we had reached so far. Everyone was quiet until the Gypsies started to talk in a very low voice amongst themselves. We didn't understand them, and therefore we didn't pay any attention to it. All we knew was that every bone in our emaciated bodies ached, and all we wanted was to be able to sit down. No food had been provided on this trip, but we didn't even miss it anymore.

Close to the Gypsies stood a group of Hungarian girls who understood their whispers. In a barely audible whisper, one of the Hungarians began to speak to one of the girls close to her who was Polish and Gentile. She, in turn, looked for someone who understood Polish and the whispers reached Rosje Klein. What the Polish girl told her was that the Gypsies had decided to murder as many of us during the coming night as it took to get enough room for them to sit down and be comfortable. Rosje spread the word in German and Dutch, all, of course, in the lowest of whispers. It is likely that these "lovely" ladies were sure that no one in this car understood what they said in their tongue or that we were aware of their intentions for the nightfall. With no room to maneuver at all, the girls closest to the Gypsies knew they'd be the first to be attacked.

As soon as it got dark, the Gypsies made their move. But being forewarned and being helped by everyone who was able to, the attacked girls could fight back and free themselves. Everybody was kicking and punching the Gypsies, twisting their arms and pulling at their long hair. At one time I lost my footing and slid down. Several feet trampled on me. Someone realized my predicament and pulled me up. The whole scene was horrible, and all during this the train went chuckling along. I don't remember how long this nightmare lasted but when the train stopped and the boxcars were finally opened, we all looked like ghosts. Ours was the only boxcar in which nobody was killed, and in that respect we were fortunate. Many, many corpses were thrown out, and then more were pulled out of the other boxcars.

A work detail was commandeered, and I was part of it. Blankets were handed out, and we were ordered to remove the bodies and carry them in the blankets some distance from the train and dump them near some woods. It was only then that we realized that where the train had come to a halt was in the middle of the Lüneburger Heide, a beautiful part of northern Germany where the purple heather grows as far as the eye can see.

We were allowed to leave the train and "camp" outside. Some food was finally brought for distribution to us, and we got some bowls and formed a line. Somebody started to ladle out whatever was in the food kettles when, suddenly, the heavens opened up and rain and hail began to pelt us. Inge and I were together in the line and with a few others left it to take shelter under the boxcars. When the storm let up, and we got back in the food line, Herta, who had become our blond Jewish enemy in Vught when she somehow started to be a Nazi puppet, told us that we had had our portion already and just wanted a second helping. She closed the kettle and with a sadistic grin walked away. I think that this, more than anything else of all the dirty tricks she had committed, made us, later in Sweden, prove her a traitor and get her convicted. Not that the little bit of soup would have made any difference, but it was her utter meanness that enraged us.

Someone came up with the idea of eating grass, which began to grow light green between the brown, dried stalks of heather. After all, we tried to convince ourselves, if a cow can eat it, why can't human beings eat it too? Somehow, someone started a fire, got some water, put the grass and water into a tin bowl that had been somehow "organized," and cooked the mess. Well, let me tell you, cows may like grass but cows have four stomachs with which to digest it. Grass sure is not for human consumption, even starving humans. The stuff tasted so bitter and awful that nobody could swallow it. Boiled leaves from some trees tasted much better. Not that those few leaves would have kept us from starving, but at least looking for the leaves kept us too busy to think and worry about what was still ahead of us.

When it started to get dark, we were ordered back into the boxcars. We were scared of the coming night, of the Gypsies and what would happen, and how many of us would survive. Again the murderous crew did its work but this time, with everyone forewarned, not as many were killed.

It was on the third day of what we came to call the Gypsy Camp that, upon getting out of the boxcars, we realized that the Gypsies had vanished. There was no trace of them, and nobody had heard anything during the night, much less seen anything, that could shed any light on their disappearance. But no one was sorry that this bunch was gone.

In a matter of two days we all had changed into ghostly skeletons, and we hardly recognized the girls with whom we had shared years in the camps. In the middle of the next night the train began to move again, and when the doors were opened, we were in Hamburg-Eiderstedt. It was on a gray and dismal day that the train pulled into a real station with platforms so that we didn't have to risk our lives and limbs jumping down from the high boxcars. We stood there, on the platform, in a long raggedy column, five deep, waiting for what would happen next. And that turned out to be so unexpected that some of us began to cry, others to laugh, and still others just stared in utter disbelief.

Marching onto the platform we were already on came some German uniforms, and the foremost among them was our old friend *Obersturmbannführer* Reinecke from Vught. He looked at us and slowly began to recognize a few of our faces. A wide grin spread across his face and in a husky voice he almost shouted, *"Meine Mädels!* [My Girls!]" He seemed happy and moved to see us again. He asked a few questions and after hearing that we hadn't eaten or slept in days, got us out of the station and into a camp as fast as he could.

Chapter 13

May 1, 1945

The camp was a dirty place. I couldn't imagine what it might have previously been used for. It certainly hadn't been built for its present purpose. Long, low, and very old buildings surrounded a large center square. On one side was a kitchen, on the other a large kind of a washroom, neither of which did us any good without any food or water. We were allowed inside immediately. There were bunks, two high, and, as usual, two of us to one bunk. We got some bread and were told that it wasn't necessary for us to go out for a roll call again, which was good news because all we wanted was some sleep.

Inge and I again shared a bunk and next to us was Betty. A year or two ago, she had found a little piece of cardboard and had fashioned a calendar out of it. She was very unhappy. She wanted to continue her calendar but April was the last month she was able to squeeze onto that little piece of cardboard. "Don't worry," I said to Betty, "we'll be liberated the beginning of May. You really don't need any more space!" I really don't know what made me say it.

Next morning we were called out for roll call, and some officers went up and down the line looking us over. Chills went up and down my spine and everyone else's, I am sure. This was very much like the selection ceremonies back at Vught, but this time they were looking for the strongest. There was nothing strong about any of us but then everything is relative. They picked about thirty or forty, who must have seemed satisfactory for whatever purpose they had in mind, including me. Next we formed a column and marched out of the camp toward the outskirts of Hamburg. The countryside was somewhat hilly, and the ground sandy. Our female guard was a not so young but rough and tough gal from Berlin. About two rows ahead of me marched a girl who had somehow fashioned herself a pair of footwear that were so weird that it's difficult to describe them. They were long pieces of cardboard folded over the toes and held together by a piece of wire. Anyway, she walked—or rather tried to walk without losing them—and they were more of a hindrance than a help. After a while, the guard said to her, *"Mensch, zieh doch die Latschen aus. Du Kannst ja so nicht loofen!"* It is hard to translate this order because it was said in that wonderful Berlin dialect which is the most humorous one I know, but it meant, "Hey, you, get rid of those 'slippers,' you can't even shuffle in them." The girl was reluctant to obey the order, but I'm sure the walking got much easier for her.

111

Our destination was a long trench that was supposed to be a tank trap. It was laid out along some probably very scientifically planned line that seemed very mysterious to us. Originally it was about 2 to 3 feet deep, and we had been chosen to deepen it to about 8 to 10 feet. We were handed shovels that I believe were heavier than we were, and told to start. At first it wasn't too bad. But soon we reached the water table, and the sand got very heavy. It was almost impossible to throw even the tiniest amount of the soggy stuff up to the rim of the trench, and our hands began to sprout blisters and hurt. Pretty soon we were standing in about 2 feet of water. Our footing was less and less sure, and the sand shifted constantly. Thus we found ourselves sitting in the water as often as we stood in it.

The ditch was very long, and we were a small group, and therefore we didn't get very far. In fact, all we dug was one pretty big hole. After about five days of this—we did get the hole a bit wider but not much deeper—we were taken to a nearby wooded area to uproot small trees and carry them to the ditch. There was quite a heap of those poor little trees lying there when several staff cars arrived, and some very high uniforms got out of them, and it soon became obvious that they were not on the friendliest of terms with each other. They walked to the edge of the ditch and got into a heated argument, calling each other *"Dummkopf,"* and worse. Finally we realized what the big dispute was all about. It was a matter of grave importance, namely, on which side of the trench the trees should be planted so the enemy tanks wouldn't be able to detect the ditch. One of the bigger wigs wanted to have them planted on the west bank, another on the east one. So, for a while, we were kept crossing and recrossing the ditch, each of us with a motley little tree in our hands. In the end it was decided to plant them on both sides, (something I had suggested under my breath to somebody about two hours earlier), and the uniforms got back into the cars and drove off. In the happy knowledge that enemy tanks were coming, we planted trees that day, and all of the next. I'm sure the ditch didn't do much good, and I'm just as sure it never did an "enemy" tank any harm either.

That evening, we were greeted, upon our return to the camp, by very sad news. We had been losing, all along, friends, girls with whom we had shared those gruesome years. We had all become more than friends, more even than family. Two sisters who had been with us almost from the beginning were especially dear to us even though they didn't "belong" to our little circle. The younger one had just gone mad that day and ran into the washroom. Shortly thereafter others went looking for her and found her on the floor dead. Her name was Anne Frank (but not the one whose "Diary" became so well-known). Our Anne had been a lovely, quiet, and highly intelligent girl who just gave up. Our bodies and minds couldn't take it anymore either. The will to live, to fight on, was vanishing fast. Still, her death shocked Bonnie, her sister, as it did all of us.

There was no food in the camp whatsoever, not for the prisoners and not even for the German guards. News came that cheese and bread were stored in a nearby warehouse. Four of us were dispatched with a female and male guards and, of course, our canine companion, Freia, the German shepherd, to pick up 400 pounds of the stuff. When we got to the warehouse we found bread and cheese alright, but the stuff had grown hair and assumed a ghastly color of green. It was completely moldy. Nevertheless four bags were filled with the spoiled food and brought back to the camp, so that we couldn't be accused of not having gone to the warehouse in the first place. Well, the very next day, May 1, 1945, we, the same quartet together with our guards, were sent out again. This time the rumor had it that there was a warehouse in the harbor filled with sausages. Off we went with our empty bags, tired legs, and high hopes.

Our camp was on the other side of the city, far from the harbor. Therefore our German protectors felt we should get permission to use public transportation. We entered a streetcar for the first time in three years. Of course, as prisoners we had to stand in front with the conductor. To our surprise the passengers as well as the conductor were most sympathetic and friendly toward us. One gentleman looked at us, smiled somewhat sadly and said, "Don't worry, soon it'll all be over—very soon!" This entire excursion gave me a strange feeling. I wasn't quite sure whether I was just dreaming. Of course, we were in Hamburg where the Nazis were never popular.

We arrived at the station at the end of the line, somewhere in the center of Hamburg, then walked a few blocks to catch a train that would take us to the harbor. Before we reached the train, the air raid sirens came alive. Close by was an air raid shelter, and we, along with what seemed like half the inhabitants of Hamburg, ran toward it. It was deep under ground and heavily reinforced with concrete, but we still could hear the muffled sounds of an enormous bombing raid. Our male guard kept begging us to please stay close together so we wouldn't lose each other, and, I'm sure, he was at this point more concerned about our safety than about his reputation as a typical German guard. When the all-clear finally sounded, and we emerged from the shelter, we could hardly recognize the place. It was just a lot of rubble. The train station was gone, and we picked our way carefully through the fallen bricks, shattered glass, along burning houses, toward what we hoped would be another station where we could pick up another train.

We did find a train, and it delivered us to the harbor after what seemed an eternity. Once there, we embarked on our search for that particular warehouse. Well, believe me, to look for a certain warehouse in any harbor is not an easy, task but if you stand in the midst of a freshly devastated harbor, then the task is almost impossible. "Almost," I said, because we did find a more or less intact warehouse filled with sausages. We didn't know whether this was the warehouse we were supposed to find but I suspect the sausage gave it away. The stuff looked very much like the cheese and bread we lugged home the day before—hairy, green, and awful. Again, we filled our bags and started back to camp. With the sausage-laden bags heavier than we were, the struggle to drag them along was an unfair one. We tried to carry them on our backs but those things kept sliding down pulling us down with them. Then we tried dragging them. Even our guards helped but our progress was painfully slow to say the least. Somewhere we picked up a streetcar that mercifully went to Eiderstedt. We climbed aboard with our bags and reached the end station about 45 minutes later. It was early evening. Had we not caught that streetcar, it would have taken us probably all night and maybe even the next day to get back to our camp. Unless, that is, we had parted company with the green sausage.

The camp was about half a mile from the terminal. Completely exhausted, we were just dragging ourselves and the bags along with no one saying a word. We must have been something like 600 feet from the camp entrance when Salli said to nobody in particular, "Funny. I see a white car

The sausage-hunting expedition.

with a red cross painted on it in front of the camp." I didn't even bother to look up and just said in Dutch, *"Ja, je ziet ze vliegen,"* which loosely means, "You're crazy." Pretty soon somebody else made the same observation, "Salli is right, there's a white car with a red cross at the camp's entrance." Now I looked up and saw it too. At the camp entrance we were greeted by a tall gentleman in a strange uniform. I truly can't remember any more what he said, but our commandant, who stood next to him, made us put our bags down, "because they were much too heavy for us," he explained. (I could have told him that before.) Then he introduced the gentleman as a representative of the Swedish Red Cross and told us that while we were on our sausage hunt, the camp had been liberated.

WE WERE FREE. It was such a strange sensation this being free. It didn't sink in until we had walked down the road toward the barracks and joined the other girls. Seeing their joy, their tears, hearing them sing and laugh finally brought it home to us—we really, truly were free.

I just sat down on one of the bunks and started to cry and couldn't stop. Betty came over, put her arm around me, and told me that I had been right, her calendar had just made it. And, like that calendar, we too just barely made it. There was little strength left, physical or spiritual, in any of us.

None of us slept that night. We were just waiting for what the next day would bring. We couldn't imagine what would happen to us, what "being free" would mean, where we would go or what we would do. We talked all night, visited the other barracks, something we, of course, had never been allowed to do before, then went back to our bunks to rest a bit.

It got light, and nothing happened. Nobody came to get us out for roll call. Nobody came and yelled at us. Nobody barked any orders. It all felt awfully strange. We had been used to following orders for such a long time, doing exactly what we were told to do—it was after all a constant matter of life or death—that now, all of a sudden, we felt kind of lost. Small groups of us huddled together on the lower bunks wondering what to do when Reinecke and the Swedish gentleman entered to tell us that we would shortly be taken to the railroad station for our trip via Denmark to Sweden and that we should get ready. We were now as ready as we had ever been for the past few years. There was nothing to pack, no farewells to say.

It was hours, or so it seemed to us, before we were finally called out of our barracks and, out of habit, we lined up, five deep, and when the gates were opened we marched out of the camp in our habitual column. In retrospect now, it was just as well that we did so. Otherwise there might have been a great deal of confusion, and things might not have gone as smoothly as they did. The march to the waiting train was something else. In those moments, not one of us really believed that the liberation was true. We were certain that we would suddenly wake up and find ourselves back in the nightmare that had been our life.

The waiting train consisted of cattle cars. The doors of the boxes were wide open, but there was a difference: a thick carpet of wonderful smelling straw was spread out on the floor and the infamous shit pail was pushed into a corner. Only forty of us to a car so that we could stretch out full length. Someone handed each of us a miniature loaf of bread and then began the most nerve-wracking wait we had endured yet. At last a guard in an SS uniform entered the car, greeted us a bit awkwardly, which was hardly surprising under the circumstances, and sat down near the door, which remained open. This could signify two things, one that we had some more waiting in store or, as we hoped, that the door would remain open during our trip. And then, very, very slowly, the train began to roll, so quietly and slow-ly that at first we were not sure at all that we were really moving. We were so used to the banging and crude jerking of the locomotives against the cars in which we had the "pleasure" of crisscrossing the country, the sudden bumps and knocks of the trains starting out that threw us against each other and the sides of the boxcars, that this slow, smooth start was a unique ex-perience. Yes, we were indeed pulling out of the station, and the door was still open.

Except for the rhythmic clang of the wheels rolling over rail links, it was very quiet in our car. A few cried, and some talked softly to each other. Most of the girls, including myself, had terrible stomach cramps. We might have had a touch of dysentery or it may have been just nerves, or both. The pail was constantly being used but now the guard emptied it every chance he got. There were short stops along the way, some at stations, some between as the train obviously was waiting for signals to change. But now, more than ever before, those stops were pure torture for us because we were still in Germany and still in the war, and we knew we could be hit by a bomb even now. Such thoughts were not conducive to calming our nerves. Daylight faded, and as night fell, we reached the Kaiser Wilhelm Canal.

I was sitting close to the open door, with my arms hugging my drawn-up legs because of the terrible stomachache, and I could see outlined against the somewhat lighter sky the darker silhouette of an enormous bridge, and we all knew that once we made it across to the other side, we would be in Den-mark. The excitement mounted. But suddenly in the middle of the bridge ap-peared a red signal and our train stopped. I will never forget the ghastly hopelessness that settled over me at that moment. Of course, once the first shock wore off, we all realized that this was just another red light, and sooner or later it would turn green, but while we were waiting there in the middle of the bridge with Denmark less than a mile away, my stomach cramps seemed to get worse. Our nervousness didn't help matters either. Our guard helped us out of the boxcar so that we could squat on the trestle and do without the pail. He held our hands, though, so that in the event the red light changed and the train started again, he would be able to pull whoever was down there back up into the car. Finally, the light did change, and slowly, oh, so slowly, the locomotive started up, and we were chucking over the rest of the bridge.

And then we saw it, a big marker. We had crossed the border!

I can't remember how long it took after our crossing the border to get to our destination, but we were now in Denmark. It was still dark when the train ground to a halt, and we disembarked at a huge flat stretch of land. On one side, an enormous tent had been erected. On the other, a long train made up of sleeping wagons stood on some sort of a siding. Half of the disembarked group was directed to the tent and the other, including our group, to the sleeping cars. The beds had been removed and mattresses spread on the floor. We tumbled into the car and onto the mattresses. The train was heated. We were dead tired. The warmth and the knowledge that we were free, and that one could get out and back into the train at will, was almost too much to bear. We were so exhausted that we finally fell asleep despite being unbelievably excited. But, alas, this blissful condition didn't last long.

The lice, evidently disliking the cold, had been dormant and thus left us alone. But in the warmth of the sleeping cars, they became quite lively and began to dance and jump on us. Every fiber in our bodies wanted to sleep, and every louse on our body had no intention of letting us do that. We were unable to get back to sleep, and we just scratched and helped each other reach unreachable places. There was really nothing else we could do but await daylight when we would be better able to deal with the lice and ask for the heat to be turned off in the cars.

The moment daylight made it possible, we got out of our rags and proceeded to hunt the lightfooted pests. In the midst of that fascinating activity, the door opened, and there entered the then Crown Prince of Denmark with a large entourage. Our *Lagerälteste*, who happened to share our quarters, got up in all her skinny splendor without a stitch of clothing on and said in German, *"Entschuldigen Sie bitte aber wir sind dabei uns zu entlausen.* (Excuse us, but we are in the process of delousing ourselves]." Whereupon the prince replied most graciously, *"Bitte lassen Sie sich nicht stören.* [Please don't let us disturb you]."

Seeing us there, living, naked skeletons all of us, must have been rather shocking to these people, but despite the real threat of infection the entourage went slowly through the train, greeting each and every one of us. Afterward they proceeded over to the large tent to greet the skeletons there.

A few hours later, we were called out for breakfast. Women in brown uniforms—"Lottas," as they were called—were standing around large steaming kettles. These women were all volunteers, from all walks of life, giving freely and lovingly of their time. How often have I thought of them and how often I feel ashamed of myself because I don't think I ever thanked any of them for all they did. I suspect that we were just too tired, too sick, too worn out to think of such civilities and I hope the Lottas were aware of that and forgave me. But I am ashamed just the same.

Anyway, the large, steaming kettles were filled with very thin and watery porridge and to this day I am amazed at the wisdom of our liberators. Knowing full well that we hadn't eaten anything for such a long time, they didn't take any chances on giving us much or heavy food. We all got a small portion of the oatmeal, and most of us couldn't even manage to eat that.

When I try to imagine paradise, I always think of the five days we spent in Denmark. We were free as we had not been for an eternity. We rested and slept and at intervals were fed. Some doctors looked us over and decided who was sick enough to be flown to Sweden to be treated in specially designed and hastily set up hospitals.

Mostly we enjoyed our freedom. The weather was mild, and the war was over, at least for us. One very important thing that we did during that time was to write a letter to the American and British authorities. In it we pleaded for Papa, detailing his decency to us and explaining how he had bent over backward and taken grave risks to help us. I truly hope that this letter helped a man who, despite the horrors around him, remained a fine human being.

At this point, of course, we did not know yet just how great our losses were but somehow that was very remote to us. Then came the day when we had to say good-bye to this beautiful spot, and we resumed our travels through Denmark in a train, a first-class passenger train, outfitted with velvet seats, and at every station along the long route were people, hundreds of people, cheering, crying, waving. Totally unlike our travels in the cattle cars. Every time the train stopped, hands offered cookies, cakes, bread, and fruit in enormous quantities, and as soon as we pulled out of the station the Lottas came along to gather up the offerings lest we should eat them and become deathly ill. I don't remember too much of this trip except that the landscape through which we traveled was magnificent, with hanging gardens and trees in full bloom.

We arrived in the port of Fredericia where we left the train and went aboard a ship for the voyage to Sjaelland. On board, we ate again, very light and thin porridge. The tables in the dining salon were set with gleaming white linen and silver, and there were flowers in the middle of each one. I suspect we were all afraid to wake up and find ourselves back again in some camp barrack. What was amazing was that we were together with civilians. We were still kept somewhat apart because of the threat of infection and the spreading of lice was enormous.

After the crossing, another train trip and then onto a ferry for the sailing to Malmö in Sweden. On that ferry, cards were handed out to be filled out by us. Name, former address etc. Now the strangest thing occurred. Almost none of us remembered her last address or the exact date of birth. We were told not to worry, that our memory would come back. All of us fervently hoped so, although I had my doubts. But the Swedish medical team that reassured us on this point eventually proved to be correct.

The author's forced itinerary detailed in this book: (1) Amsterdam to Vught; (2) Vught to Auschwitz-Birkenau; (3) Auschwitz to Reichenbach; (4) Reichenbach to Trautenau; (5) Trautenau to Porta Westfalica; (6) Porta Westfalica to Beendorf; (7) Beendorf to Lüneburg; (8) Lüneburg to Eiderstedt; (9) Eiderstedt to Malmö. Spelling according to contemporary usage.

We disembarked at Malmö on a cold and gray day. The wind made the brown uniforms of the Lottas flutter as they stood by tall kettles filled with very bitter cocoa. We all had to drink a cup, and then we were taken to buses which drove us to a huge Swedish shower. We undressed there and put our clothes in a pile to be burned. One girl took her shoes off for the first time in many months. I don't know how she had gotten hold of those shoes, but once she had them she never took them off for fear of having them stolen. The soles of the shoes stuck to her feet, and it took soaking to remove them. To her surprise, there were two one hundred pound notes, one in each shoe. The former owner must have hoped to buy if not freedom then maybe some food. Those two bank notes were such a sad and pathetic sight! So futile! But as a result of that find, we went through the pockets of our discarded clothes and felt along the seams and under linings. Here and there we found valuables, a pair of earrings, a necklace, some more money. It was painful to find these little treasures, the only remnants of those who had hidden them.

We were asked if there was anything we wanted to keep before it all was burned. Yes, I had the little wrench in my hand, the one that saved my life when the glass window and wall came crushing down on me in Reichenbach. I had become very attached to it. It was my talisman, and I was allowed to keep it after it was thoroughly sterilized. Following this search party, we were taken to an enormous bath with immense shower heads all over the ceiling. Women, protected from head to feet in rubber suits, started to wash and scrub us with large soft brushes and nice smelling soap. The warm water on our bodies felt wonderful, and the feeling of being cared for was indescribable. We were then rubbed dry with large towels and our now somewhat grown hair was sprinkled with some anti-louse powder. Blue coveralls, wooden shoes, and a kerchief were waiting for each of us. Once we were dressed, we were brought to a long and large room where we came face to face with a battery of doctors whose combined expertise covered every part of our anatomies. They took turns in looking into our throats, ears, and noses. Others stabbed us and listened to our lungs. In short, they checked everything that was checkable. It took a long time for us to be finally released, and by then it was already dark outside. But it was dark with a difference. For the first time, after all those dark years, we saw light in windows. Lighted billboards, and traffic lights.

There was light outside, and there was light in our hearts. But, alas, there was much darkness in our souls, and it would take us many years to cope with it. And some of us never could.

Epilogue

The time in which my story played is slowly fading into history, and yet the story itself becomes ever more sharply etched upon the consciousness of men. I have lived with my memories of that time for so many years now that they have become a part of me. Since my liberation, I have tried to prevent those years—during the war and in concentration camps, where fear was my constant companion—from influencing my life, my actions and my disposition.

I know that many of my Holocaust cosurvivors find it hard, and some even impossible, to come to terms with that episode in their life. Some are immersed in it or constantly dwell on it while others have completely erased those years from their psyche and memory thus losing that period of their lives.

Many of the friends who shared the years of that nightmare with me are no longer with us. Too many died of cancer. Some, like myself, were able to restart and even resume a normal life again.

I realize that I am one of the lucky ones who have been able to absorb the Holocaust and, thus with the years, found my perspective and tolerance enriched.

After my liberation I stayed one year in Sweden, then I came to America where I met and married a wonderful man with whom I had two fine sons, both now happily married and raising families.

When my sons were too young to burden them with something so utterly dreadful as the Holocaust, I began to write down my memories of that terrible time in my life.

Those memories are just that, and they might differ from those of my fellow compatriots whose perceptions of identical events are colored by their characters and personalities. Siblings growing up in the same household with the same parents can have memories that are, in fact, poles apart.

I felt strongly that my sons should, in time, come to know and understand as fully as possible those years which interrupted my life and why I, their mother, was sometimes different from other mothers.

But, most importantly, I wanted them to learn that life could be rough, and that one could survive rough spots provided one had an inner strength, was self-reliant, did not take oneself too seriously and tried never to lose a sense of humor.

It began as a journal, which, after many years of neglect, grew into a book.

When a close friend, Alex Urban, a veteran editor, read the manuscript, he thought that it deserved an audience extending beyond my children and friends. I am indebted not only for his unwavering support but also for assisting me in crafting this book in its present form.

Of the many memorable individuals with whom I shared the experiences described earlier, I should single out the following:

Dr. Kohn came to the United States where she was a professor at Harvard until her death of cancer several years ago.

Inge came to the United States, and then moved to Israel, where her health has declined with age. Her innate sensitivity was severely impacted by her experiences in the concentration camps and her love of classical music helped her cope with her brutal past.

Sally's postwar life, besides her earlier Nazi era experiences, was filled with enough drama and twists to make a separate story. She also came to the United States where she got married and had a son. She died recently of cancer.

Paula went to Israel where she settled down to a reasonably normal life, replete with a husband and children. She continues in relatively good health.

Lotte of the long legs came to America, married a professor, and died of cancer several years ago.

I wish I could conclude my epilogue with some sense of assurance, or just hope, that the world and its inhabitants, the new generation and the generation that will follow have learned from our devastating experience. I wish the slogan "NEVER AGAIN!" would have meaning and the world would act accordingly.

But to my deep sorrow I know now that our suffering did teach humanity that the tolerance toward atrocities and bestiality seems limitless. Human suffering at the hands of fellow humans is continuing as if there had never been such a thing as THE HOLOCAUST.

The End